my favourite things

Simply The Best
Edited by Vivien Linton

First published in Great Britain in 2009 by:

Young Writers
Remus House
Coltsfoot Drive
Peterborough
PE2 9JX
Telephone: 01733 890066
Website: www.youngwriters.co.uk
All Rights Reserved
Book Design by Tim Christian
© Copyright Contributors 2008
SB ISBN 978-1-84924-080-2

Foreword

Young Writers' My Favourite Things is a showcase for our nation's most brilliant young poets to share with us the things they appreciate most in life.

Young Writers was established in 1990 to nurture creativity in our children and young adults, to give them an interest in poetry and an outlet to express themselves. Seeing their work in print will encourage them to keep writing as they grow, and become our poets of tomorrow.

Selecting the poems has been challenging and immensely rewarding. The effort and imagination invested by these young writers makes their poems a pleasure to enjoy reading time and time again.

Contents

Mohammed Irfan (12)	1
Jasmine Jones (11)	2
Feyi Kadri (10)	3
Jack Zuliani (12)	4
Owen Palfreyman (12)	5
Charlotte Mullinger (11)	6
Eden Fashoyin (11)	7
Jermaine Wilson (11)	8
Sian Davies (9)	9
Tilly Jayne Fox (11)	10
Kayleigh O'Connor (12)	11
Jessica Barrett (8)	11
Olivia Barnett (10)	12
Jessica Bridgman (9)	12
Lucy Hoyle (13)	13
Victoria Cane (10)	13
Sian Leighton (10)	14
Danielle Banks (12)	15
Lewis Bluck (10)	16
Emma Hamilton (12)	17
Karla Caesar (11)	18
Sam Coombes (10)	19
Rowan Drury (12)	20
Jade Addy (11)	21
Erica Constantine (10)	21
Emily Cossey (10)	22
Joe Lewis (8)	22
Daniel Longe (12)	23
Lucy Payne (11)	24
Faye Allonby (8)	24
Rebecca McGlone (9)	25
Bethany Wardle (11)	25
James Brotherston (11)	26
Jack Meakin (12)	26
Alex Stephenson (11)	27
Elena Leddy (8)	27
Maesie-May Edwards (8)	28
Laura Powell (12)	29
Lucy Hudson (8)	29
Owen Whelan (13)	30
Alice Davies (12)	30
Heather Broome (13)	31
Lucy Jennings (8)	31
Victoria Reynolds (11)	32
Danielle Juden (13)	32
Abbie Pearson (12)	33
Emily Darville (8)	33
Mathilda Bassnett (9)	34
Alice May Davies	34
Hayley Moore (12)	35
Libby Ashcroft (7)	35
Jade Blagg (13)	36
Juliet Soane (9)	36
Abigail Elliott (11)	37
Courtney McKelvie (10)	37
Madison Webb (12)	38
Emily Perry (14)	38
Leena Zafrani (12)	39
Martine Vrieling van Tuijl (9)	39
Bronté Whitlock (13)	40
Jusleen Kaur Gill (9)	40
Emily Farrow (12)	41
Mitchell Krence (9)	41
Salma Perveen (13)	42
Courtney Leigh Penman (11)	42
Alice Marshall (9)	43
Paige Russell (12)	43
Patrick Williams (15)	44
Mohammed Ahmed Riaz (10)	44
Matthew Hoskin (13)	45
Lauren Kingston (8)	45
Olivia French (12)	46
Katie Roberts (12)	46
Laurie Cabbin (10)	47
Fleur Gascoigne (14)	47
Emily Bourlet (10)	48
Louise Bell (11)	48
Angharad Moran (8)	49
Sean Stillman-Jennings (9)	49
Amy Rhodes (12)	50
Emma Satterley (10)	50
Jessica Nikolla (10)	51
Whitney Kneen (13)	51
Fathima Ahmed	52

Name	Page
Sophia Dalla Costa (12)	52
Rebecca Sharp (11)	53
Georgia Williams (7)	53
Sugitha Pathmanathan (12)	54
Sophie Ward (7)	54
Chloe Knott (9)	55
Georgia Porter (9)	55
Harriet Maslen (11)	56
Kane Barker (10)	56
Precious Orji (11)	57
Victoria Wuche (10)	57
Jamie-Leigh Flintoft (10)	58
Rayne Hill (13)	58
Aisha Yasmine Sesay (11)	59
Courtney Farley (10)	59
Leah Leonardi (9)	60
Bethan Evans (11)	60
Ben Wilders (9)	61
Kirsty Bishop (11)	61
Victoria Evans (13)	62
Nishath Jarin Pushpa (10)	62
Jessica Gray (12)	63
Olivia Loizides (12)	63
Zainab Hussain (9)	64
Samra Ibrar (8)	64
Jennifer Hornal (11)	65
Deborah Adewale (10)	65
Beth Coxon (10)	66
Asha Gilbert (11)	66
Maria Walley (10)	67
Dusty Mason (10)	67
Jack Barker (12)	68
Tamzin Stallard (10)	68
Rakim Sajero (10)	69
Alex Dougall (8)	69
Cara Mathews (12)	70
Rebecca Sheldon (11)	70
Ellis Martin (11)	71
Amber Walker (11)	71
Georgia Welch (12)	72
Carolina Valensise (9)	72
Hannah Kelso-Mason (13)	73
Michelle Saunders (10)	73
Hayley Hughes (11)	74
Keshav Bhardwaj (10)	74
Chloe Roberts (12)	75
Hannah Voss (11)	75
Rosie Reville (10)	76
Hasnain Ali (10)	76
Louise Jesi (11)	77
Cressi Sowerbutts (11)	77
Nicole Roberts (Batty) (12)	78
Sophie Mallen (11)	78
Klara Prela (9)	79
Robin Hannay (8)	79
Alison McAliece (9)	80
Keshini Gooneratne (14)	80
Charles Gibbons (11)	81
Chelsea Kelly (8)	81
Luke Dawes (11)	82
Hannah Clifford (11)	82
Athnah Justus (10)	83
Paige James (10)	83
Anisa Zahid Fazil (11)	84
Bethan Wood (10)	84
Chloe Warburton (10)	85
Georgia Walther (8)	85
Cassandra Boyce (11)	86
Amy Clarke (13)	86
Anusia Battersby (11)	87
Ailsa Knight (9)	87
Abigail Swift (12)	88
Jade Armer (14)	88
Aaliyah Jordan (11)	89
Holly Griffiths (10)	89
Rachel Hollingworth (10)	90
Josephine Ruiz (10)	90
Sophie Cook (11)	91
Katy Hodgson (10)	91
Maisie Wilders (7)	92
Siobhan Bailey (9)	92
Alicia Jones (9)	93
Jack King (14)	93
Steven Baird (10)	94
Rachael Pippen (14)	94
Grace Mitchell (13)	95
Hannah Brown (13)	95
Anne Dillon (13)	96
Bethany Hinds (12)	96
Tyler Booker (12)	97
Aimee Davies (10)	97
Emma Williams (11)	98

Deborah Mills (11) 98
Trevor Tooth (11) 99
Charles Woolhouse (11) 99
Curtis Hannington (10) 100
Chantal Kaufman (11) 100
William Shepherd (10) 101
Eleanor Morgan (10) 101
Vanessa Nakitende (11) 102
Tiegan Flynn (10) 102
Karsha Brown (10) 103
Emily Price (10) 103
Sabina Saleem (11) 104
Zulaikah Patel (11) 104
Kaelan Wade (12) 105
Chloe Murray (10) 105
Molly Burford (12) 106
Wendy Su (12) 106
Sanka Edirisinghe (11) 107
Rebecca Pendry (10) 107
Remel Enyioko-Bakers (12) 108
Lara Howells (10) 108
Emily Jones (12) 109
Thaniya Miah (12) 109
Wayne Perks (13) 110
Thea Wormald (8) 110
Sarah Freitas (12) 111
Joel Hall (10) 111
Samantha Foxon (11) 112
Kara Allen (9) 112
Olivia Rose Wanless (8) 113
Joya Sastry (12) 113
Tasnima Khan (14) 114
Shaun Whelan (11) 114
Zaki Thomas (9) 115
Albert Perris (10) 115
Ruqia Jaan (10) 116
Emily Darling (11) 116
Paige Blake (13) 117
Shannon Gair (12) 117
Georgia Rochester (9) 118
Samantha Lee (9) 118
Simone Thomas (11) 119
Georgina Morris (11) 119
Nicole Olivia Dallison (9) 120
Sarah Venters (13) 120
Khowla Shahid (11) 121
Hadley Whiting (10) 121

City of London School for Girls
Athen Brady.................................. 122
Rose Pitman-Wallace (8) 123

The Poems

MY FAVOURITE THINGS - Simply The Best

Yeah, Sure

As old as it may seem
As grey as it may be
It wasn't clean
And it simply cried, 'Play me'.
I remember the times we had
It was bought for me
By my dear old Dad
I nearly cried, I was immensely happy
A never-ending game
A 3D puzzle or maze
My life will never be the same
While I play, with a transfixed gaze
I placed my hand upon the controller
I marvelled and stared in awe
As I was told to behold her
I'd never experienced something so cool
Alas, it had come to an end.
All the games, the money I'd spent
For what I ask myself?
That collection upon the shelf?
It happened all of a sudden
With a snap, fizzle and pop
It was evil, such a cruel bludgeon
My PlayStation, it was silenced, at a stop!
I became desperate
I was going mad!
I didn't get it repaired
I had to ask my dad
Dad will you buy me another?
The PlayStation2, it's special, brother!
'Why, yes son,' he replied
My horror was rectified
So there we have it my fellow comrades
This poem was about PlayStation and cool dads
As good as they may seem!
Just remember to keep them clean!

Mohammed Irfan (12)

All About Jazzy

Walking, talking
Strutting my stuff
Make-up and glitter
It's just a bright flicker

Drawing, scoring goals
And playing roles
I love textiles
And all different reptiles

Playing footie is fun
And most of all I love to run
Shopping is cool
And splashing in the pool

I love to dance
Street, tap and modern
It keeps me fit
So I don't feel rotten

I love pink,
And all things fluffy
But most of all,
I hate getting mucky.

Scouting For Girls
Is my best band
Sugar Babes and Basshunters
Are also around

Playing with my rabbit
Hop, skip and jump
Eating ice cream
And hearing Snowy
Go *thump, thump, thump!*

CDs are the best
And I really don't mind tests
I love taking pics
And playing different discs

MY FAVOURITE THINGS - Simply The Best

Roller coasters and rides
I love
But when it comes to high ones
I've got no luck

Louise, Ellie and Nicola
These are a few of my friends
They are crazy, just like me!

Jasmine Jones (11)

Me, Myself And I

Skipping to school and going to class,
Choir, country and Scottish dancing,
Playing with my friends and whispering in lessons,
Going on trips, especially Hall Green.

Flopping on the chair on a Friday night,
Watching movies and eating popcorn,
Saturdays I wake up very late,
Never, ever wanting to get out of bed,
Sundays, going to church, singing songs
And praying to God.

Christmas, really hoping snow will come,
And eating turkey, Yorkshire puds and the whole lot!
Birthdays, getting lots of cards, parties and presents!
Easter, getting eggs, chocolate and more chocolatey things!

Watching TV, getting lost in my *favourite* programmes,
Reading books, staying up late and
Asking Mum for more books,
On the computer writing books
And adding them to my collection.

Putting gloss on to go to parties,
Be the belle of the ball!
Hanging out with my friends
Eating pizza and chips!

Getting a hug from Mum and Dad,
And watching X Factor,
Shouting out who should go home.

Feyi Kadri (10)

Your Favourite Thing!

I like drama, but in time.
I like English because I like to rhyme.
Although music's not my best,
I always like a hard test.
I like the dates in history
And jumping around in PE.
Although theses are my favourites,
I also play the violin and sing.
Is this your favourite thing?

Out of school I have a blast,
Half-term, school's in the past.
Playing on my Nintendo DS,
No time to have a rest.
Listening to my MP3,
No time for rugby.
I have to live for my sport,
Football's my best, or so I thought,
Until I came across rugby,
And oh, you'd better watch out,
I do karate.
Places to go and things to do,
Visit the pub and go to the zoo.
Go and watch my team play,
Go to the fete and have a great day.
Spy on my brother, creep and lurk,
Go to the library to do some work.

Getting presents on special days,
Trying to work in different ways.
Watching the nativities,
Chewing sprouts and crunching peas.
Eating food and chewing gum,
Buying presents for my mum.
Will she like a golden ring?
Is this your favourite thing?

 Jack Zuliani (12)

MY FAVOURITE THINGS - Simply The Best

Family

My most favourite thing that I enjoy the most
And enjoy it every day,
Is going out with family,
Going out to play.

Fishing with my uncle,
And playing with my bro,
Taking Nana's dogs for a walk
Because I have one so.

My dog's name is Misty,
He's a rabbit-hunting pup,
But he could catch a pheasant,
That's if we have the luck!

Making bonfires with step-dad Paul,
And making treats with Mum,
Sharing them out with my family
And hearing them all say, *'Yum!'*

Oh I do love Bonfire Night,
With fireworks to see,
But the one thing I enjoy the most
Is being with family.

Putting masks on with my little brother,
My brother's a lovely lad,
Then creeping round to Nana's house
And scaring our grandad.

Oh I do love Hallowe'en,
But there's something I love more,
And that's being with my family,
And that's all I'm here for.

Owen Palfreyman (12)

My Favourite Things

My favourite thing is to jump in the sea
And sometimes to drink ice-cold tea.
Another thing is to do arts and crafts,
But also to have lukewarm baths.
My favourite thing is doing PE
And at the end scraping the mud off my knee.
My favourite thing is to have lunch,
But also having an apple to crunch.
I love so much to cook,
But also to read a good book.
My favourite thing is dancing,
Which sometimes involves prancing.
I sometimes like to sing
And listen to the doorbell ring.
My favourite thing is my cat, Twinkle,
And I feed her a tuna sprinkle.
My favourite thing is my friend, Annie,
But she has a really weird granny.
My favourite thing is going to the park
And also playing games in the dark.
My favourite thing is going on a cruise,
But I really hate getting a bruise.
My favourite thing is leaping into the sea,
Like a dolphin, wild and free.
My favourite thing is climbing trees
And looking at the honey bees.
My favourite thing is going to the zoo
And watching the monkeys say *boo*.

Charlotte Mullinger (11)

My Favourite Things

Playing on my Nintendo DS and on the run,
Playing with my friends, having so much fun.
Going to birthday parties,
Going on holiday in the scorching sun.

Watching films on the TV,
Playing on my grandma's Wii,
Eating vegetables that are good for me,
But having sweets and ice cream, going to sleepovers,
Playing with my next-door neighbours.

Playing Scrabble with my family,
Designing clothes, doing something handy,
Going shopping, picking out clothes and foods,
Well that's what I like to do.

Computer games, funky gadgets,
Playing football, volleyball, basketball
And also tennis, athletics and gym.

Going to school, doing science,
Making experiments and explosions,
Using tools in design and technology,
Doing art, but not biology.

X Factor, singing, dancing, steel pan,
Violin, keyboard and music,
Having a laugh when I do my thing.

Let me just say one more thing,
These are all my favourite things!

Eden Fashoyin (11)

Sports, Games And Music In Challenge

Football, football is my dream,
Football, football is a game I love,
When I score a goal my mum likes to scream,
Now you see why I love football.
It's a game I like
And football is its name.
I think I'm really good at it,
And I hope I'll be in the hall of fame.

Tennis was always my sport,
So much drama and passion.
I love watching them play,
I want to be like Roger Federer,
The king of tennis and fashion.
I never hit any stray balls,
I'm really good on the tennis court.
People love to watch me play,
Now you know why I love the sport.

These are the games I love,
They are Xbox 360 and PS3,
Now you see why I like playing them,
But baby, the games aren't free.

Another thing I like to do is play my guitar,
When I flick those strings and chords
It makes so much music.
Everyone I know loves to watch my play it,
But my favourite guitar has always been acoustic.

Jermaine Wilson (11)

MY FAVOURITE THINGS - Simply The Best

My Alphabet Favourites

A bba, the pop group
B ags, sparkly and bright
C hocolate and Christmas
D resses, drama and dancing all night
E aster eggs and bunnies
F ood, family and friends
G od, trees and green fields
H annah Montana sets the trends
I ce cream and ice skating both are great
J am and jelly that wobbles on a plate
K ites' bright colours, soaring high in the sky
L ollipops and lipsticks that catch the boy's eye
M ums are cool and very kind
N ovember fireworks and Nintendo games on my mind
O ven-hot pizza, playing in hot sunny sand
P arents and parties, with McFly as my big bang
Q ueens and kings are very loyal
R eading their books makes me feel so royal
S trictly Come Dancing and singing with glee
T aking my first dance step, not falling on my knee
U p stage with Zoey 101
V ery much is my dream number one
W inning the lottery and starring on a show
X -Factor contestant, I wish to give a go
Y es is the answer to all my favourite things
Z ooming on my new laptop would make me feel like I had wings.

Sian Davies (9)

My Favourite Things

When I see a cute puppy, I think of my favourite things
The sound of High School Musical stars who can sing
These are a few of my favourite things.

Curled up with an interesting book
Why don't you come and take a look?
These are a few of my favourite things.

Family days out with my mum and dad
These make me so happy and glad
These are a few of my favourite things.

Christmas Eve, waiting for presents, all wrapped up with gold
These make me smile so please be told
These are a few of my favourite things.

Sleepovers with my friends
Making cute little dens
These are a few of my favourite things.

Build-A-Bear workshop
Gosh, I never want to stop
These are a few of my favourite things.

Chocolate is my kind of heaven
I could eat ooh, at least seven!
These are a few of my favourite things.

So whenever I get upset
I think of friends I have met
And remember that these are my favourite things.

Tilly Jayne Fox (11)

MY FAVOURITE THINGS - Simply The Best

Favourite Things

Going to town with all my friends,
Keeping up with all the new trends.
Going on the PS2,
Playing 2 Vs 2.
These are the things I like to do.

Listening to my alarm clock beeping,
While I am sleeping.
Playing rounders,
But in the break I eat my quarter-pounder.
These are the things I like to do.

Watching basic cable,
Then going to the stable.
Chocolate and sweets are the best treats,
Walking along the beach, hearing all the seagulls screech.
These are the things I like to do.

Go to birthday parties,
Eating all my Smarties.
Playing with pets,
Watching them run and collect.
These are the things I like to do.

Watching snow fall,
As I play football.
Putting up the Christmas tree,
While parents drink their tea.
These are the things I like to do.

Kayleigh O'Connor (12)

Mr Cheese

He's small and fluffy, my Mr Cheese,
He reminds me of Muffy, my Mr Cheese,
He rolls fast in his ball, my Mr Cheese,
He pouches his treats, my Mr Cheese,
My favourite animal's my Mr Cheese,
I do hope he doesn't freeze, my Mr Cheese.

Jessica Barrett (8)

Running

Running for school,
Running for the city,
Running in the mud
Can be very tricky.

Wearing spikes
And my Stoke Athletics vest,
I always try
To do my very best.

Running up a hill,
Running through a stream,
It's a great way to keep fit
And to run off steam.

When my mum shouts,
It sounds like a scream,
I always run well,
But coming first is a dream.

I even love running
When it's cold and wet.
My coach, Bill, says,
'I haven't seen the best of you yet!'

Running for fun,
Or running for a medal,
It does not matter which,
Because running is special!

Olivia Barnett (10)

There Was A Girl From Bangkok

There was a girl from Bangkok
Who wore very big socks
She climbed a wall
Ten feet tall
The amazing girl from Bangkok.

My favourite things are countries!

Jessica Bridgman (9)

MY FAVOURITE THINGS - Simply The Best

A Bunch Of My Favourite Things

There are many things I like,
Including riding a bike.
But I cannot list them all,
So here are some; in a pattern they fall:

I love to talk when I'm not allowed
And I enjoy being the centre of the crowd.
It is fun learning to play the drums,
So I go to a hut and play with my chums.

I really, really like to read
And I can do so at a speed.
Oh, I also love to write,
But I totally hate Turkish Delight!

I'm not too sporty, but I love PE,
But I'm definitely not good at IT.
Aren't assemblies such a drag?
We already know that smoking is bad.

I like Lego, 'cos I love to build
And I'll eat chocolate till my tummy's filled.
I love to dress up in my dressing up clothes,
But everyone groans when I put on my shows!

Me, I live in a fantasy land,
If you were me, you'd understand.
I love my life and the way I look,
In the near future, look out for my book!

Lucy Hoyle (13)

Butterflies

A pretty, little butterfly, sitting on a leaf,
Her colours are so pretty it is hard to believe.
I see a little boy with a jar in his hand,
Waiting very quietly for the butterfly to land.
So please little butterfly, quickly, quickly fly away home,
Because I don't want the jam jar to be your new home!

Victoria Cane (10)

Favourite Things

Laughing and joking with my friend,
Sometimes I wish it would never end.
We have such fun when we are together,
I hope we stay friends forever.

Kicking my ball across the grass,
My friends all think I am first class.
Scoring a goal in the back of the net,
No other person is a threat.

Hallow'en, time to trick or treat,
Going around houses for something to eat.
Give me a trick and I'll egg your house,
Give me a treat of a white chocolate mouse.

Making stuff out of glitter and glue,
Sometimes even cooking, too.
There are lots of things I like to make,
Maybe even baking a cake.

Playing with my friends in the snow,
Playing until I'm numb and sore,
Then coming in and warming up
With my hot chocolate in my favourite cup.

Opening my presents on Christmas Day,
I love them all in a different way.
Eating my veg and meat for lunch,
With all my family, we are a great bunch.

Sian Leighton (10)

Magical Moments

Frost on a newly-spun spider's web,
Glistening in the morning sun.
Like a lace embroidery made by silver thread -
Now we know his hard work is done.

Fresh snow on the bare branches of trees,
Adds a touch of colour to the land,
Wrapping the world in a comforting white blanket -
We don't mind holding it in our hand.

The glow of a sunset on a summer's night,
Reflects beautifully over the sea,
Turning everything into a myriad of colours -
It's like a special kind of magic to me.

The warmth of a pup after he has played,
Snuggled up close for his nap,
As worn out and tired as a newborn baby -
I'd hold him fast asleep on my lap.

The cheeky behaviour of the chimps as they play,
Makes you want to stay and watch forever,
Chasing each other and playing the fool -
Do we behave like that, no! never!

The soft, velvety feel of the fur on a seal,
Its sorrowful eyes pull at your heart strings,
Making you giggle at his rippling blubber -
These are a few of my favourite things.

Danielle Banks (12)

My Favourite Things

My favourite things are for all to see.
The great, big, open, roaring sea
I know some dogs called Milly, Molly, Mandy,
They're very good but don't get any candy.

I go to school and play with my mates
And after that I lift some weights.
My favourite thing at school today
Was doing art and playing with clay.

I have a favourite book,
Called How To Get A Fish On A Hook,
I have another book,
Called How To Cook.

My favourite time is playing with my mates,
We love to jump the garden gates.
But when it rains, it's such a pain,
It soaks us through to the brain.

I love to go on a hike
And to take my favourite bike.
It's small like a trike
And my shoes are made by Nike.

I have lots of favourite things you see,
Computers, toys and cups of tea,
Building stuff is my thing.
What is your favourite thing?

Lewis Bluck (10)

MY FAVOURITE THINGS - Simply The Best

I Thought . . .

I thought of this, I thought of that,
I thought of coats and shoes and hats.
I thought of trains and teds and dolls,
I thought of hats and scarves and balls.

I thought of skates, I thought of mates,
I thought of cats and dogs and plates.
I thought of pizza, I thought of pasta,
I thought of spinning, faster and faster.

I thought of ropes, I thought of Mum,
I thought of chewing, chewing gum.
I thought of sister, I thought of Dad,
I thought of all the fun we'd had.

I thought of birds, I thought of planes,
I thought of lots of fun and games.
I thought of books, I thought of cars,
I thought of money and gold bars.

I thought and thought of what to write,
But the paper looked so very white.
I thought of animals, I thought of pens,
Ah - I'm going to write about my friends.

My friends are my favourite thing,
They make me want to jump and sing.
They make me happy when I'm sad,
They make me very, very glad.

Emma Hamilton (12)

All About Me

Everyone loves something,
Like playing on the swings,
However, these are a few of
my favourite things.

High Street fashion,
Makes me feel great,
Or should I go designer,
So I can show off to my mate?

Going to a sleepover,
Having a midnight feast,
Telling scary stories,
With a man-eating beast.

Eating home-made cooking,
Chicken, rice and peas,
When the soup comes out,
It's always, 'Seconds, please.'

Going on a roller coaster,
Hurtling down perilous peaks,
I'm so petrified,
I can barely speak!

Everyone loves something,
Like playing on the swings,
However, these are a few of
my favourite things.

Karla Caesar (11)

My Joys Of Live

My favourite things
Are singing and drums,
For a dentist maybe,
Searching your gums.

My favourite things
Are school and work,
For some people,
Driving their Merc.

My favourite things
Are flying my kite,
On the computer,
And riding my bike.

My favourite things
Are the snow and sun,
My favourite sandwich
Is ham on a bun.

My favourite things
Are nature and life,
And searching the woods
For a king and his wife.

My favourite things
Are on the beach,
My favourite fruit
Is a peach.

Sam Coombes (10)

My Favourite Things

Drawing and dreaming,
Being with my friends,
Thinking and talking
Setting new trends.

Music and make-up,
Having a laugh,
Eating milk chocolate,
A long bubble bath.

Parties and dancing,
Watching TV,
Shopping and sunsets,
Being by the sea.

Reading and writing,
Smelling a rose,
Wearing long dresses
And designing clothes.

Glitter and glamour,
Mist over lakes,
Stars and sparkles
And freshly-baked cakes.

Slides and seesaws,
Going on swings,
These are all of
My favourite things.

Rowan Drury (12)

My Absolute Favourite Things

My absolute favourite things
Most definitely have to be
Playing in the snow,
Always being on the go,
Drawing funny things,
Pretending I had wings.

My absolute favourite things
Most definitely have to be,
Having a lie in,
Imagining I was a mermaid, with a colourful fin,
Eating a chocolate cake,
Preparing to bake.

My absolute favourite things
Most definitely have to be,
Going swimming,
Watching my brother giggling,
Being creative
As well as persuasive.

My absolute favourite things
Most definitely have to be,
Playing with the girls,
Doing great big twirls,
Going for a hike,
Riding my bike.

Jade Addy (11)

Playing

P laying with my friends all day long,
L ying on my bed, singing songs.
A hug from my mum I would miss,
Y awn as I awake from my perfect kiss.
I love chocolate, especially white,
N ight-time, sometimes, I get a fright.
G oing now, bye-bye.

Erica Constantine (10)

My Favourite Things

I love sport,
When I go to a court
I can't even stop to say naught.

I love being outside in the sun.
When I am eating a bun,
I can't wait to play when I'm done.

I love to be with my family every day.
Especially when we lay
In the garden in May.

I love all animals, even cats,
I especially like tigers and I even like bats,
But none of these animals likes to wear hats.

I love my friends,
I colour in, using my pens
And I make cosy dens.

I love to swim, I'm just like a fish,
I'd rather go swimming that eat food on a dish,
I wish I could breathe underwater, I just wish.

I love to read,
I would read anything, not even for a bead
And I don't read just to do a good deed.

I also love dancing and acting!

Emily Cossey (10)

Football

Football, football, a lovely, crazy game.
I like to play on a sunny, cold day.
Picking the team can be very, very hard,
We might be lucky and end up with Jimmy Bullard!
Pass. Pass. Pass. I need to score,
I want to be the champion for ever more.
Foul throw, corner kick, *goal!*

Joe Lewis (8)

MY FAVOURITE THINGS - Simply The Best

The Joy Of Christmas

Jingle bells, jingle bells,
That's the song of the day.
The sweet smell of turkey,
Stuffed, on the table it lays.
The bright light everywhere,
Like God has made,
This is a day of presents
And of joy, we hope will never fade.

Before we eat we see the crackers,
Dancing on the table.
We grip them tight and pull,
Then *bang!* the gift falls out.
Sweet smell of turkey stuffing,
With a hint of Brussels sprouts,
Filtered back into my nose,
All was good and all was edible.

After we feast on that glorious meal,
We head for the grand finale,
The presents is the little spark
That brings us all to Christmas parties.
As you've read, my wonderful poem,
You now know the reason
Why my emotions turn around
When it comes to the Christmas Season.

Daniel Longe (12)

My Ten Favourites

Dancing is a hobby, I haven't done for long,
It is great fun and we dance to different songs.

My room is one of them, where I relax and rest,
I play and watch TV and it is the best.

Lumpy is a favourite, he is an old teddy bear,
I had him when I was little,
I love him and give him great care.

I love summer, it's so fun,
I play with my mates and enjoy the sun.

I also like winter, even though it is chilly,
We build snowmen and make them look silly.

My birthday is great, I am another year old,
It is in winter, so it is very cold.

I also like cooking, especially chocolate cake,
They are so yummy and tasty, that why I like to bake.

I love to eat sweets, also ice cream,
They taste so great, it is my dream.

My favourite meal is chicken al forno, that's what I like to eat,
Also favourite is Sunday roast, with vegetables, potatoes and meat.

My last thing is colouring, it is great to do,
With colours of pink, green, yellow and blue.

Lucy Payne (11)

My Favourite Things

My favourite thing is TV
Maybe it
Might also be
Chocolate,
Drawing,
Teddies.
I really think is should be
Chocolate!

Faye Allonby (8)

MY FAVOURITE THINGS - Simply The Best

What Is My Favourite Thing

What is my favourite thing?

My favourite thing could be so many things,
My Xbox, television or my diamond rings.
My shoes, my clothes, my make-up set,
Or my puppy, my special pet.

What is my favourite thing?

There are so many things.
So much to do,
I'll think of a thing
And give you a clue.

What is my favourite thing?

It could be thick or thin.
Square or round
And it may weigh more than a pound.

What is my favourite thing?

Have you got it yet?
It's really good,
You could read it by yourself if you could.
So go on, have a look,
My favourite thing is my story book.

That is my favourite thing!

Rebecca McGlone (9)

My Favourite Things!

Nintendo games and playing in the sun,
Visiting friends, and holidays are fun.
Playing in the garden, catching things with wings,
These are a few of my favourite things!

Christmas is the best,
Better than all the rest,
Celebrating the birth of Jesus, King,
These are my favourite things!

Bethany Wardle (11)

25

These Are A Few Of My Favourite Things

XBox and playing football,
Even though I'm not too tall.
Scoring a goal in the back of the net
And meeting up with friends I've already met.

Best of all, I desperately want a dachshund dog
And going for a healthy jog.
I love X Factor and reading a Roald Dahl book
And going fishing and catching a fish at the end of a hook.

I love holidays and having fun,
Especially bathing in the scorching sun.
I love parties and exciting things to do
And hamsters and helping animals for me and you.

I love laptops, friends, animals, family and Westlife,
I hope when I grow older I'll get a wife.
I love exercise and people say I'm good when I sing
And I love wrestling when they're fighting in the ring.

I love to watch Celtic, Scotland and the Scotland rugby team play.
And when they win I shout hooray!
I love chocolate, toffee and treats,
But most of all I love sweets!

I love theme parks and making stuff out of paper and glue,
I have shared my favourite things with you.

James Brotherston (11)

Untitled

PlayStation games and computers
All my favourite things.
But I don't have a laptop, so I really hope this wins.
X Factor and Strictly Come Dancing,
Watching all those people sing.
Diana to Rachel, to Alexandra,
All good singers,
Who is gonna win?

Jack Meakin (12)

MY FAVOURITE THINGS - Simply The Best

Now That I'm Older

When I was little I played with my rattle,
Now that I'm older, I take my Warhammer figures to battle.
When I was little, Thomas the Tank Engine I used to see,
Now that I'm older, I watch lots of other TV.
When I was little I loved mashed banana and orange juice,
Now that I'm older, I much prefer roast chicken with gravy sauce.
When I was little I used to go to sleep with my dummy,
Now that I'm older, I fall asleep reading my book called 'The Mummy'.
When I was little the entire world was my mum,
Now that I'm older, it's the playground and my best chum.
When I was little the wheels on the bus went round and round,
Now that I'm older, hard rock is the only sound.
When I was little I loved driving my little *broom-broom* car,
Now that I'm older, I wanna be a rock star.
When I was little I cuddled my teddy bear,
Now that I'm older, I apply gel to my hair.
When I was little I thought dressing up as a pirate wasn't odd,
Now that I'm older, I've swapped the sword for an iPod.
When I was little I played rough and tumble with my daddy
Now that I'm older, I get plenty rough playing rugby.
We kids grow up and change, and so do our favourite things.
One thing's for sure, though,
Favourite things make us all feel like kings.

Alex Stephenson (11)

Hula Hoop

Hula hoop, hula hoop
Oh what fun!
You can do it in the sun.
All you do is swing it round,
You can find some with a weird sound.
My favourite ones come in all purples,
You can even get some shaped like turtles.
Now can you see what a hula hoop is to me?

Elena Leddy (8)

All About Maesie-May Edwards

I have so many favourite things
That I don't know where to start.
When I saw the competition
I thought, *why not take part?*
I love my chocolate fountain, it is yummy,
It makes lots of lovely swirls in my tummy.
I go in the garden, where my brothers are playing,
Then I burst in with my water gun and start spraying!
If I had a dog it would be my favourite too,
Although my little brothers would probably
Call it something silly, like Doodle-Doo!
There is nothing better than my comfy, warm bed,
It makes it comfy for my little blonde head.
I adore my holidays, we sometimes go to Spain,
Although my ears go *pop, pop, pop* on the plane.
Christmas is one exciting and sparkling time of year,
And at New Year's Eve it is a special time to cheer!
My friends are fabulous, they mean a lot to me,
So as I like to cook, I invite them round for tea.
Now we've come to the end of my favourite stuff,
There's so much to choose from, it's been quite tough.
I hope you've enjoyed learning the special things about me,
Now I am off to another favourite,
Fajitas and nachos for my tea.

Maesie-May Edwards (8)

My Favourite Things

My favourite things, how can I choose?
Not one of these things would I like to lose.

'Walkies' and 'Holidays' I just love to hear,
And the sound of my owner's footsteps coming near.

The rattling of keys is so exciting,
Please let it be my favourite outing.

The smell of roast chicken, oh how I adore,
No matter how many times I'm told, I won't leave the door.

Seeing the beach makes my heart fill with joy,
Chasing my red ball; it's my favourite toy.

As yummy as gravy, I chew my bone,
The taste is scrumptious, just like an ice cream cone.

Being touched by my owner, stroked with her love,
Then when I stretch for my basket it's like Heaven above.

Feeling the warmth of my owner's right palm,
I realise it's only her that makes me feel calm.

I'd lose all these favourites to exchange for just one:
The best owner ever under the sun.

So when she whispers, 'You're my favourite pup ever,'
I know nothing will part us, now and forever.

Laura Powell (12)

Fun Stuff

I love reading in the sun
And having fun
Skipping,
Skip, skip, skip
And having parties
And a huggy from my mummy.
I go swimming,
Play badminton and tennis
And they're fun.

Lucy Hudson (8)

My Favourite Things

My favourite things, as you shall see,
Turn out to be just one,
As football is the only thing for me.

I race home from school,
I'm nobody's fool.
I pick up my ball in the yard,
A few kick-ups here, a header there,
Then I boot it really hard.

The garage door is my goal,
And it hits hard with a *bang,*
Then rolls back to my boot,
Where it began.

I support a team called Man U,
As I'm sure loads of others do.
Rooney joined up and went far,
Then look at Van der Sar.
But I have to say, Ronaldo can play
And he is the best by far.

In my dream I join the team
And one day you'll see
Some other kid send this in,
And instead of Ronaldo, it's me!

Owen Whelan (13)

My Favourite Things About The Beach

The sight of the white sand, as pure as newborn baby's skin
And the crystal blue waters that ripple like silk.
The sound of waves lapping gently against the rocks,
Stroking them in the sun as they slowly but surely wear them away.
The smell of sea air, fresh and crisp, cool and cleansing,
The taste of sea salt on my tongue,
A flavour that is sweet and bitter at the same time.
The feel of warm sunbeams that reflect like glitter on the clear water
That is full of fish that make a living rainbow.

Alice Davies (12)

My Favourite Things

Computer games and sunbathing in the sun,
Visiting family and friends and them giving you a bun.
Watching TV and munching onion rings,
Are these a few of your favourite things?

Birthdays and Christmas presents and shows,
Watching the X Factor and feel the tension grow.
Playing football with my mates
Painting butterflies, especially their wings.
Are these a few of your favourite things?

Parties and eating ice cream and sweets and playing with a pet,
Doing my face and hair, with my make-up set.
Doing loads of shopping and buying fancy rings.
Are these a few of your favourite things?

EastEnders and reading a really interesting book,
Making beans and toast and scrambled egg,
You will be surprised how much you can cook,
Listening to a CD and dancing along when the people sing.
Are these a few of your favourite things?

Doing well in maths and adding up all the sums,
Eating your favourite fruit, especially a plum.
Having no shoelaces, then making them out of strings.
Are these a few of your favourite things?

Heather Broome (13)

Arts And Crafts

Folding across the dotted line,
Trying hard not to get it wrong.
Smoothing down the coloured card;
Its soft feel on your hand.
Cutting out pictures from glossy magazines
And sticking them onto paper.
Painting on canvas, writing and drawing,
Cutting out pictures and sticking them on,
I love arts and crafts.

Lucy Jennings (8)

A Few Of My Favourite Things.

My dog and going for a jog,
Talking on the phone,
Walking home, alone,
Listening to the microwave ping,
These are some of my favourite things.

My big brother, my pretty mother,
Playing on my Nintendo DS,
Writing letter with a PS,
In the choir listening to the triangle ting,
These are some of my favourite things.

My PlayStation 2,
My brand new pair of shoes,
A Christmas tree,
A nice cup of tea,
I believe in good luck,
I like to play with strings,
These are some of my favourite things.

My TV and watching a DVD,
Flowers and very big towers,
My dad and being very, very mad,
On TV hearing about spring flings,
These are some of my favourite things.

Victoria Reynolds (11)

The Best Things In Life Are Usually Free

The best things in life are usually free,
Playing down the park, gym or PE.
Riding my bike around a hill or a tree,
Skiing in the garden when it's cold and icy.
Playing a card game and winning, *wee hee!*
Winding up my sister, but no that's not me.

The best things in life are usually free,
But my favourite thing of all must be,
Snuggling in my bed, just me and teddy!

Danielle Juden (13)

My Favourite Things

Playing out with my friends,
Having such a laugh,
Six weeks have begun,
Now lets have some fun.

School has ended,
Summer is coming,
Camping in the garden,
Whilst telling scary stories.

Staying up late,
On a two-day sleepover,
Me, Sammie, Ellie,
Watching the Saturday's on telly.

Thinking about sweets,
While doing our makeovers,
Going up the park
To meet some friends of ours.

Oh no, school's back,
Got maths, English,
Science, what a drag!

So that's just a few of my favourite things,
I'll do a lot more and see what Christmas brings.

Abbie Pearson (12)

Untitled

Chocolate is chunky, like my dad,
Chocolate is funky, like my mom.
Chocolate is smooth, like my brother,
Chocolate is sweet, like my sister.
Chocolate is comforting, like my nan,
Chocolate is fab, like my grandad.
Chocolate is nice, just like me,
Chocolate is naughty, just like my dog.

Chocolate is my dream.

Emily Darville (8)

My Favourite Things

My favourite teddy is Poppy,
Her ears are really floppy.

I like to practise my singing
And to hear Santa's sleigh bells ringing.

I love to practise my dancing,
My feet just can't stop prancing.

I love to eat ice cream,
It always is an absolute dream.

I would love to have a bunny,
Even though they cost a lot of money.

My favourite friend is Leah,
Her dad drinks lots of beer.

My favourite shop is the Bear Factory,
I go there every month, naturally.

I love to see cute babies,
Luckily they don't have rabies.

My best subject is art,
I love it so much more than dark.

These are all my favourite things.

Mathilda Bassnett (9)

Favourite

F is for flowers, smelling so fine
A is for apples, taste so divine
V is for voles, so cute, so sweet
O is for ocean, the waves on my feet
U is for umm, my favourite sound
R is for roundabout, goes round and round
I is for ice cream, with sprinkles and flakes
T is for timetable, school is so great!
E is for everyone, including me
    These are my favourite things that you see!

Alice May Davies

MY FAVOURITE THINGS - Simply The Best

My Favourite Things

Seeing my friends, every day
Going on holiday far, far away.
Playing with jewellery, pretty, gleaming rings
These are a few of my favourite things!

Playing with my gorgeous cat, Smudge
Or eating a bit chocolate fudge.
Hitting the shuttle cock with my badminton racket strings
These are a few of my favourite things!

Watching TV, Corrie is the best
Going to bed for a rest.
Learning about historic queens and kings
These are a few of my favourite things!

Reading a Jacqueline Wilson book
Trying to learn how to cook.
Dancing and prancing when Katy Perry sings
These are a few of my favourite things!

Scoring a goal with the ball
Sledging in the frosty snow, trying not to hit the wall
Christmas and birthday, opening my presents and treats
These are all of my favourite things! -
but don't forget those tasty sweets!

Hayley Moore (12)

Is That Fun For You?

Making stuff out of coloured paper and glue,
Is that fun for you?
Laptops and gadgets and playing with your pets,
Is that fun for you?
Hallowe'en and Christmas and having fun scoring a goal,
Is that fun for you?
X Factor and reading a good book,
Doing something cheeky, then let off the hook.
Smiling when Girls Aloud or McFly sing,
Are these a few of your favourite things?

Libby Ashcroft (7)

My Favourite Things

Just a few of my favourite things
Include dark chocolate and purple violins.
Listening to music in peace and quiet too
And of course, Eeyore, Tigger and Winnie the Pooh.

Reading a really great book
That gets me excited.
Drinking a nice, hot chocolate,
That makes me delighted.

X Factor and Strictly on a Saturday night,
The nerve-wracking results give me such a fright!
Not forgetting a mouth-watering Chinese,
Duck, pancakes, sweet and sour chicken balls,
That'll do for me.

But my favourite of all, brace yourselves, are you ready?
Going down to the theatre on the night of birthday
With Mum and Dad and grandparents too,
Watching my nanna giggle as the witch says *boo!*

Just being with my family
And watching a really great play
Is my favourite thing of all,
That really makes my day!

Jade Blagg (13)

Favourite Things

Swimming and gym and dancing,
Laughing, running and prancing,
These are a few of my favourite things.
Creating, parties and dressing up,
Drinking out of my favourite cup,
One of my favourite things is to sing,
Computers, playing, hugging my mum,
Eating, jumping and sucking my thumb,
I'd like to have a diamond ring.
These are all of my favourite things.

Juliet Soane (9)

MY FAVOURITE THINGS - Simply The Best

My Favourite Things

Dogs wagging tails and being with friends
Dad being silly and gym on weekends
Mum going shopping, nice treats that she brings
These are a few of my favourite things.

My hamsters, running and chasing about
Teasing my sister and making her shout
Watching X Factor when a bad person sings
These are a few of my favourite things.

On holiday with family, playing cards round the table
Riding a pony then back to the stable
Racing my sister to the phone when it rings
These are a few of my favourite things.

Playing a football match and scoring a goal
Making cakes with Mum and licking the bowl
Playing my guitar and plucking the strings
These are a few of my favourite things.

When it's bedtime,
Falling over
When I'm feeling mad.
I simply remember my favourite things
And then I don't feel so bad.

Abigail Elliott (11)

Favourite Things

My favourite things are for you all to see,
The flowers, the birds, the plants and the trees.
When you look out of your window at night,
You see the stars and the moon shining bright.
But how would you feel if that was all gone,
When you would have nothing then to look upon?
I see us people recycling at last,
So let's look to the future, forget the long-suffering past.
Some kids want chocolates but that's just not me,
Cos all I want really is this planet to last for eternity.

Courtney McKelvie (10)

37

You're A Special Mum

I wrote this poem from me to you
To say that I love you.
You're thoughtful and kind
And very gentle too,
You're fun and happy
All the year through.
You make me happy
When I am feeling down,
You're very clever
And I am proud.
So come over here
And give me a hug,
It will make things better
And I will understand
That you're the greatest mother
Of all the land.
Everyone loves you
And I do too.

Lots of hugs and kisses
From your baby girl
To you.
Xxx

Madison Webb (12)

Being Me

What is my most favourite thing?
It is doing my very own thing.
Not having to worry about fitting in,
I don't need the latest thing.
I only do what I want to do,
Not what somebody has told me to.
Following the crowd,
Just ain't my scene.
What makes me proud
Is being me!

Emily Perry (14)

MY FAVOURITE THINGS - Simply The Best

Seasonal Activities

Autumn's around the corner, so time to stay indoors,
Watching TV, playing games and so much more,
DVDs, hot chocolate and eating ice cream,
Watching football and supporting my favourite team.
These are a few of my favourite things.
As winter comes it's all fun and games

As winter comes it's all fun and games
Snowmen to make 'cos Christmas is here again.
Snow-fights and snow-angels, with laughter all around
Ice-skating with friends and falling to the ground.
These are a few of my favourite things.

When spring is here, nature blooms,
In my spare time I redecorate my room.
Picking flowers and making a daisy chain,
Spring showers come and I play in the rain.
These are a few of my favourite things.

Finally, summer has arrived to stay,
Going to a theme park or a nice holiday.
Swimming, dancing and playing in the sun,
Sunbathing, relaxing and having lots of fun.
These are a few of my favourite things.

Leena Zafrani (12)

The Sea

I was walking along the shore
When a beam of light struck my eye.
All I could see was sparkling sea
In front of me.
The sky lit up and the birds
Flew over my head.

Little heads pop up from the sea,
One by one they look at me.
As the sea rises, the sun goes down,
It's time to get into my dressing gown.

Martine Vrieling van Tuijl (9)

Jessica

I'm sure people own things that they really love,
Which may be as white as a dove,
Or as warm as a glove,
As cuddly as a bear,
Maybe too good to share,
But I own something that inspires me most
And before I go on, I don't mean to boast!
My favourite thing I see every day
And I must say,
That by the way,
I didn't have to pay.
She stands on four paws,
With very blunt claws,
Wags her tabby tail
And does almost everything without fail.
When I return home from school
I look down to see something small.
I wonder what's wrong
Until she purrs round my feet.
I understand she would like something to eat.
I don't know how to express myself more,
But she is the cat I adore!

Bronté Whitlock (13)

My Favourite Things

F un in the sun, with my friends,
A movie with adventure,
V ideos that fill your mind with happiness,
O rigami, boxes, birds and much more are fun to make.
U ncle and Auntie staying for Christmas.
R ings, necklaces and all types of jewellery.
I ce cream of all flavours.
T asty sweets and food.
E specially when my favourite things are given to me.
　　But my favourite thing is my family.

Jusleen Kaur Gill (9)

My Favourite Things

Getting it right, the fur on my feline,
The warmth of the flames, the chill gone from my spine.
The wind through my hair as I'm flapping my wings,
These are a few of my favourite things.

Passing the bakers on a cold, windy day,
Smelling the first flower in the middle of May.
A sweet, soapy scent that a bell from Lush rings,
These are a few of my favourite things.

The bitter and the tangy, the hard and the chewy,
The taste of sticky toffee, all delectable and gooey.
Put a taste in your mouth and the dreams have no endings
These are a few of my favourite things.

The smile on your face, tears bleeding the eye,
The underwater mysteries of blue, pink and green.
The pattering and waddling of small, fuzzy ducklings,
These are a few of my favourite things.

The loud shriek, the ringing of the Friday bell,
The freedom to go and escape from this cell.
Frosty town filled with season's greetings,
These are a few of my favourite things.

Emily Farrow (12)

Favourite Things

I like to dream about Christmas,
About all the nice things Santa brings.
I like Christmas if it snows,
But will it? who knows?
As I write my letter to Santa
I get a tingle in my tummy.
I like football,
I like my toys.
So when writing the letter,
Remember,
Santa only brings toys to good girls and boys.

Mitchell Krence (9)

My Seasonal Joys

The flowers begin to bloom in spring,
My heart swells as I hear the birds sing.
Whilst we clean the dust so that the sun will pour
Golden rays that make us gape in awe.

Summer arrives, with water guns and pools,
Children giggle with glee as they leave their schools.
Time for ice cream, games, visits and going shopping,
For gadgets, clothes, stickers and perhaps a key-ring.

I'm crunching the leaves now that autumn is here,
Will we be watching the fireworks this year?
Squirrels scurry around us, we buy gifts and decorations,
For birthdays, Hallowe'en and other occasions.

In winter we huddle beneath the Christmas tree,
Sharing chocolates and food and watching telly.
It is great to have a party and shuffle in snow,
Or think about other things that I enjoy so.

These are the things that I favour and like,
From a hug from my parents to riding a bike.
In all weathers I appreciate all of these things,
But what I like best is to share them with other beings!

Salma Perveen (13)

My Favourite Things

My Nintendo DS and the PC,
My mobile phone and that suits me.
Dancing to music and watching TV,
Having fun is good for me.
The beach and the park,
Is where I like to be,
Especially with my friends and family.
Reading a book or writing a poem,
Or even just being at home is fine by me.
I always love to sing,
So these are a few of my favourite things.

Courtney Leigh Penman (11)

My Favourite Things

Burning sunsets, all orange and bright,
Twinkling stars that live through the night,
Sparkling fir trees that give Christmas light
And clouds that make pictures at a tremendous height.

Aeros and Wispas that bubble on my tongue,
Cadbury's Caramel that stays on my thumb,
Twixs and Twirls that make me go ummm,
And Curlywurlys that make me have fun.

Horses and ponies that run through the breeze,
My Westie, Jock, that I sometimes tease,
Fluffy, wild bunnies that come bouncing in threes,
Golden buttercups that make me sneeze.

Birds that fly through the sunny sky,
Driving through rain with the music up high,
Sweeties and sundaes that I like to buy,
Wacky ribbons and bows that I can tie.

Playing music on my violin strings,
Bouncy balls that go *ping, pong, ping,*
Dragons with tails and scales and wings,
These are all of my favourite things!

Alice Marshall (9)

My Favourite Things

Playing in the garden and visiting good friends,
Going to parties and going out at weekends.
Getting up for school, getting dressed,
Doing my make-up and doing all the rest.
Getting everything ready for this big night,
All the fireworks going off in the light.
Everyone watching with such delight.
Going out for Hallowe'en, going out with friends,
Getting dressed up and playing pretend!
Christmas with presents under the tree,
And listening to tunes on the TV.

Paige Russell (12)

My Favourite Things

Xbox 360 games and diving in the pool,
Visiting family and keeping it cool.
Going on holiday, riding something with wings,
These are a few of my favourite things.

Hallowe'en and Easter - trick or treat,
Playing football and scoring with my feet.
Going to school, me and my friends thinking we're kings,
These are a few of my favourite things.

A big hug from my mum, a big kiss from my dad,
One of the favourite memories ever had.
Or that memory where my mum and dad bought rings,
These are a few of my favourite things.

Playing with my friend's baby pet,
Scoring an overhead kick, watch it go back of the net.
Harry Potter and friends eating sweet strings,
These are a few of my favourite things.

Watching Britain's Got Talent and reading a mint book,
Doing something bad, then grinning as you're let off the hook.
Laughing when my best friend sings,
These are a few of my favourite things.

Patrick Williams (15)

Having A Swim

Having a swim.
It is never dim
And keeps you slim,
It is a great treat
That softens your feet.
Pools, all shapes and sizes,
Come as great surprises,
Diving underwater with air above
And swimming with love,
You feel like a flying dove,
It's good to be off the ground and around water.

Mohammed Ahmed Riaz (10)

44

MY FAVOURITE THINGS - Simply The Best

The Things That I Like

If you're wanting to know what makes me smile
Then here is a list of those things
You can try it yourself, it's worth your while
To discover the joy that it brings.

Being out on the golf course and putting for par
Or a new game to play on the Wii
The squeal of a wheel on a really fast car
And dipping my toes in the sea.

Football with my mates, in a school holiday
And the freedom that hangs in the air
Not having to listen to what people say
And better, not having to care!

The warm, summer sun in the middle of the year
Or the snow on the ground at the end
Or listening to sounds that are pleasant to hear
Regardless of if they're the trend.

And so, that's my list, but that's not all there is
Yes, there's plenty more that I could add
So write one yourself and if you're a whizz
You can rhyme to the end of your pad!

Matthew Hoskin (13)

My World

I like music and my guitar is pink,
You could say I am a babe, but that would stink.
I like writing but sometimes the ink is gone.
I like playing with my friends
Especially when they hold hands.
I go to Brownies every Thursday night
And on Hallowe'en we all have a fright.
We all dress up scary, but there was one little fairy.
At school my friends are cool,
My brother runs around like a fool,
Not really!

Lauren Kingston (8)

My Favourite Things

Sitting in the garden on a hot, summer's day,
The pink buds opening, they've come out to play.
Kicking up the leaves, yellow, orange and red,
A snowy winter's morning and breakfast in bed!

Learning facts about long, long ago,
Acting and drama, putting on a show.
Writing poems and stories, I never can stop,
Blowing up chemicals to make them go *pop!*

Walking Nan's dog and pony rides,
Stroking my hamster, even though he bites.
Watching my cat laze around in the sun,
She's seen a butterfly, 'Run, Suki, run!'

Hanging out with friends, watching TV,
Building sandcastles, paddling in the sea.
Swimming and bowling with my family and friends,
Parties and sleepovers, the fun never ends!

Sweet treats and chocolate, savoury snacks,
Pasta and curry and spicy Nik Naks,
Peanuts and biscuits, duck and green beans,
These are a few of my favourite things.

Olivia French (12)

Hockey Wednesday

Hockey is my favourite sport,
I do it every Wednesday,
I play it with my friend,
We stay and play until the end of the day.
We play when it's wet and cold,
When you are on the hockey pitch
You need to be brave and bold.
Bold enough to score a goal,
Careful not to fall,
Hit the ball and let it fall,
Into the goal!

Katie Roberts (12)

MY FAVOURITE THINGS - Simply The Best

Laurie's Favourite Things

Flowers and butterflies, roses and tulips,
Hip hop and rap are my style of music,
The happiness and joy that my family brings,
Are these a few of your favourite things?

Sunday dinner, known in its own special way,
As people eat it on Christmas Day,
Birthdays and Christmas presents, like rings,
Are these a few of your favourite things.

Ria, Chelsea and Molly,
My friends who are so jolly.
Time for playtime, the bell goes *ding*,
Are these a few of your favourite things?

Jacqueline Wilson's so good book,
Getting latest fashion, looking off the hook,
Summer, autumn, winter, spring,
Are these a few of your favourite things?

Glittery clothes, a perfect fit!
Hip hop dancing, I want to do the splits!
Perfume that smells, my bling,
Are these a few of your favourite things?

Laurie Cabbin (10)

What I Like To Do

I sit in my room hours on end
On my laptop, talking on MSN,
But that's not all, there's other things to do
Like cut up paper, print and glue.
I go to town, into all the shops,
Picking up jumpers, trousers and tops.
I'm very energetic, I love to do sports,
Rallying the ball on the tennis courts.
When I get home I turn on the TV,
I pick up the remotes and play on the Wii.
These are my favourite things.

Fleur Gascoigne (14)

Just A Few Of My Favourite Things

What do I enjoy the best,
That makes anything
Better than the rest?
What would I choose first?

How about flying away
To have fun on holiday?
Having fun at the sea,
Enjoying laughter, you and me.

Staying home and having fun,
Fun in the garden in the sun,
Watching fluffy clouds go by,
Birds that chirp, fly and fly.

Relaxing by the hot, warm fire,
Smells of warmth go higher and higher.
Watching TV,
Or just thinking about me.

Drawing a picture,
Painting a star,
You can have fun,
Whoever you are!

Emily Bourlet (10)

My Favourite Things

My favourite things include -
Teddy bears and yummy food,
Pink Smarties and Haribo Rings,
My hamster, Hammy, the Ting Tings,
Watching my favourite shows,
Sparkly jewellery, presents with bows,
The twinkling bright stars at night,
Bags and flying kites,
Sitting in the sun,
Laughing, joking, having fun.
These are my favourite things.

Louise Bell (11)

MY FAVOURITE THINGS - Simply The Best

Stuff I Like Doing

I like reading about queens and kings
I like watching funny things
I like playing computer games
And I love watching 'You've Been Framed'.

I like chocolate and I like sweets
I like dancing to funky beats
I like playing with my friends
And I love stories with fabulous ends.

I like playing in the park
I like fireworks when it's dark
I like playing in the sun
And I love my skateboard, having fun.

I like the Jonas Brothers, they're really cool
I like also High School Musical
I like Liverpool, they're my favourite team
And when they score I start to beam.

I don't much like vegetables at all,
I don't like shopping in the mall
I really don't like doing chores
And I hate homework because I get bored.

Angharad Moran (8)

Video Games

I like playing on the PS2,
Ninja Warriors and Scooby-Doo,
Racing cars around the track,
Flying planes and shooting back.
I like playing on my DS Lite,
I'm the Hulk, let's have a fight.
Brain Train, me I'm 72,
Lego Star Wars, love it, *whoo!*
Mum gets mad when I ignore,
Then life really is a bore.
Nintendo Wii? Boy, I wish!

Sean Stillman-Jennings (9)

Happy Hobbies!

Dancing and singing I love to do,
Being on stage, meeting a superstar or two.
On TV, wearing glamorous rings,
These are a few of my favourite things.

Art, science and history are alright,
Because doing my school work makes me so bright.
Playing the guitar and plucking the strings,
These are a few of my favourite things.

Shopaholic, yeah! That's me,
Shop just like that, 1,2,3.
Make-up, clothes, shoes and rings,
These are a few of my favourite things.

Christmas and birthdays, parties with family and friends,
Candles and confetti, it really depends.
Big presents or small presents, whatever people bring,
These are a few of my favourite things.

A sunny day or a rainy day, although I do prefer the sun,
Playing mini-games and competitions, yay, I've almost won.
Viewing animals, especially those with wings,
These are a all of my favourite things.

Amy Rhodes (12)

These Are Things I Love And Do

Playing in the snow and running free in the sun,
Visiting my bestest friends and hugging my mum,
These are a few of my favourite things.

Hallowe'en and Christmas presents and more,
Skipping, singing and flying a kite, and being a good friend,
These are a few of my favourite things.

Britain's Got Talent and reading a jolly good book,
Playing with my pet, Joey, and having some fun,
And these things I love and do.
Happy New Year to you.

Emma Satterley (10)

MY FAVOURITE THINGS - Simply The Best

Love It Or Hate It

I love to go to parties
I hate to go to school
I love to look fashionable
'Cos then I'll look cool

I love to go shopping
I can do it all day or night
But the thing I really hate
Is to get into a fight

I love to dance and sing
In a group or on my own
I also love gossiping
For ages on my phone

I love my family
But only like my friends
All the girls in year 6, St Joseph's
Our friendship never ends

I love to design different things
And model them too
Not things that have just come out
But things that are just new.

Jessica Nikolla (10)

Parties Are My Favourite Thing

Christmas and birthdays and special occasions,
Going to parties without invitations.
Looking nice and going shopping for new clothes
And then partying hard when no one knows.

Christmas Day is the best time of year,
With snow as deep as a river, but no one really cares.
Snowballs and snowmen, as round as my dad,
Presents so big they won't fit in my bag.

I don't know where to start,
Because these are my favourite things.

Whitney Kneen (13)

My Fave Things!

In my diary I have a special page
In which my fave things are listed, stage by stage.
My diary is private but I suppose I can share,
But there are certain things my heart won't bare!

I love staring at guys with dreamy eyes,
That's a secret I won't disguise.
Make-up isn't really my thing,
But when I party, boy do my eyes bling!

I prefer football to makeovers and trainers to boots,
You can call me a tomboy, I don't give a hoot.
I don't mind getting dirty or getting rough in fights,
But my mum thinks I should be wearing heels and tights!

I find school cool, and reading too,
Science is my favourite, what about you?
I'm happy at school, my friends are fab,
Aaron, Ryan, Muzz, Ash and even Brad!

I'm not a net person, I prefer to text,
I love watching movies, Jason Statham's the best.
There are a few things I care to express,
But the rest of my diary I won't confess!

Fathima Ahmed

My Favourite Things

Shopping, chocolate. Pink diamond rings,
Apples, mangoes, sour tangerines,
Friends, Christmas, movies and sweets.

Sleepovers, holidays, parties and fun,
Milkshakes, dancing, Disney Channel
And beaches in the sun.

YouTube, Harry Potter, acting and singing,
Good books and jewellery that looks bling!
Eating lovely food, joking around with a mate,
Listening to Britney and staying up late.

Sophia Dalla Costa (12)

My Favourite Things

My favourite things
Are ice cream and jelly,
Sitting on my sofa
And watching the telly.

Eating chips,
All salty and hot,
Planting flowers
In a colourful pot.

Granny's jam tarts,
All yummy inside,
Playing on the beach
And watching the tide.

I love babies
In their prams,
Fluffy white sheep
And their tiny lambs.

I like seals
And fish from the deep,
But the thing I love the most
Is my sleep!

Rebecca Sharp (11)

My Best Things

Sweets and biscuits, chocolate cake
Stirring and mixing, learning to bake
Getting dirty and playing in mud
I'd like to stay that way if I could.

Singing and dancing, making up games
Pretending and acting and making-up names
Swimming, running and jumping for fun
Skipping in the rain or the sun.

These are the things I like to do
I'm so glad that I have shared them with you.

Georgia Williams (7)

My Favourites!

My favourite things are
Hearing birds sing,
I wish to have their wings.
Watching flowers bloom,
Never to gloom.
Observe little insects,
Look through the index.
Collecting leaves,
Respect beliefs.
Going on a walking journey
Very far.

My favourite things are
Reading books,
Helping to cook,
Watch television,
Go on a mission,
Drawing nature,
Watching and learning about creatures,
Going to school,
Swimming in the pool,
Eating sweets from a jar.

Sugitha Pathmanathan (12)

My Favourite Things

Chocolate is delicious, chocolate is fun,
Chocolate is nice, especially in my tum.
Brown and white, yummy as can be,
Plenty to buy for you and me.

All shapes and sizes, no matter what,
You can even enjoy chocolate when hot.

Chocolate ice cream, chocolate mousse,
Chocolate milkshake and chocolate juice.
Chocolate's my favourite, as you can see,
Come and try some and get a bar free!

Sophie Ward (7)

MY FAVOURITE THINGS - Simply The Best

Things I Like

Dancing and prancing is my favourite thing,
I love to hear the school bell ring, ring, ring.
I love to talk to my mates,
I like to help scrub the plates.
Do you like these?

My sister is my best friend,
We play and it never ends,
Then, when it's bedtime, off we go,
My little sister likes to snore.
Are you like this?

Fruit and veg I love to eat,
A yummy steak, sirloin is my favourite meat.
Strawberries and cream are my dream,
Bananas and custard, I would scream.
Would you eat these?

Sorry, I need to go,
I will come back soon you know.
I'm sure strawberries and cream
Are waiting for me, in my dream.
So a cheery, cheerio!

Chloe Knott (9)

A Few Of My Favourite Things

Hamsters, dogs and chocolate sweets,
Pasta, noodles and lots of treats.
These are a few of my favourite things.
Lemonade and reading Jacqueline Wilson books,
Movies with pirates, but not Captain Hooks.
Holidays in the sunshine and out with my friends,
Keeping up to date with the latest trends.

I can't think of any more,
My fingers are getting very sore.
So I hope you liked my poem and now it ends,
Back to keeping up with the latest fashion trends.

Georgia Porter (9)

 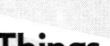 

My Favourite Things

My favourite things in spring are:
Easter, eating chocolate eggs,
Everything coming to life
And the start of a new year,
These are my favourite things in spring.

My favourite things in summer are:
Going on holiday, sun, sun, sun!
Having a break from school
And seeing my friends, having fun outside,
These are my favourite things in summer.

My favourite things in autumn are:
Having my birthday, presents, presents, presents!
Catching and walking through leaves
And the lead up to Christmas,
These are my favourite things in autumn.

My favourite things in winter are:
Having Christmas, more presents,
Getting together with the family
And having the end of a great year!
These are my favourite things in winter.

Harriet Maslen (11)

My Favourite Things

Football, laptops, running, jumping
And playing with my friends,
These are a few of my favourite things.

DS, PSP, Xbox
And eating cheese,
These are a few of my favourite things.

Lying under the sun
And having fun!
These are a few of my favourite things.

Kane Barker (10)

MY FAVOURITE THINGS - Simply The Best

Sharing My Thoughts

Snowball fights and opening presents,
Arsenal games, my birthday and Heaven,
Eating chocolate, presents I get,
Jacqueline Wilson and basketball games.

Snoozing in bed on a cold winter's day,
The lights on the Christmas tree, the snow and the hay,
Splashing in puddles, doing my hair,
Sometimes it's unfair.

I like clouds in the sky, the birds that fly,
Wind in my hair, girls on the stairs,
Children and chips and licking my lips,
These are a few of my favourite things.

Basketball and movies, chocolate and smoothies,
Ice cream and popcorn, bunnies and rubies,
These are a few of my favourite things.

Chicken and chips with ketchup and Fanta,
Noodles and broccoli and nice Coca Cola,
Fruit and cream cakes with water and soda,
These are a few of my favourite things.

Precious Orji (11)

Favourite Lucky Dip

Waking up with sunlight in my eyes,
Looking out of my window as the sun starts to die.
Chocolate biscuits and tasty treats,
Coming home from school and my room's neat.
Me, alongside my Bella bear,
When my sis ruffles my hair,
Staying up late on a Friday night,
Sneaking into bed at 3am feels so right.
Friends, sleepovers and private jokes,
Boys in the playground ready to provoke,
This is some of my favourite stuff,
For me these will always be enough!

Victoria Wuche (10)

Mum

She is a:
Chocolate lover,
Sweet giver,
Crazy shopper,
Sandwich maker,
Homework helper,
Radio singer,
Bath runner,
House cleaner.

Kid waker,
Bedroom tidier,
Curtain drawer,
Washer upper,
Bed maker,
Crazy texter.
Footy sad,
Netball mad,
Not a little bit bad,
I'm so glad
I have a fantastic *mum*.

Jamie-Leigh Flintoft (10)

A Few Of My Favourite Things

Playing football, having fun,
Horse riding and cuddling Mum.
Shopping, partying, laughing out loud,
Hyper all day round.
Singing, dancing, jumping up and down,
Swimming, cycling, exercising!
Playing guitar really loud,
That makes the world go round and round.
Listening to music and head-banging,
Reading books and writing poetry,
Writing songs, *ra, ra, ra,*
I think like a star.

Rayne Hill (13)

MY FAVOURITE THINGS - Simply The Best

My Favourite Things

I like the yellow sunrise that starts in the sky,
How it winks and speaks to the sea below.
The sea is like a river of blue magic hair,
It bashes and crashes on the gold sand.
These are a few of my favourite things.

I love the way the moon swims in the sky
And the bright stars sing along.
The nature below plays and dances and sleeps
In the dark of the day,
Red roses open their wings and spread their magical perfume.
These are a few of my favourite things.

The snow spins and twirls and lands down like mini ballerinas
And the evergreen grass spreads out its arms to hug them.
The little bugs crawl around like ancient explorers.
These are a few of my favourite things.

The yellow tiger sunflower smiles at my friends and family,
It waves goodbye with its emerald leaves.
Its long neck stretches to the sun, knowing it will get there some day.
These are a few of my favourite things.

Aisha Yasmine Sesay (11)

My Guitar

I love playing on my guitar,
It's my favourite thing, by far.
I play on it every morning,
And I never find it boring.
On Thursdays I take it to school
For my guitar lesson. That's cool!
I will play on it forever,
In all different kinds of weather.
I dream to play one day on the telly,
I hope I can go there with my friend, Ellie.
If my fingers hurt that's still OK,
Everybody is proud when I play.

Courtney Farley (10)

The Things I Enjoy The Most

P laying with my skipping rope,
I ncoming letters, I hope,
N ever not playing with a toy,
K icking footballs into goals, shouting with joy.

L istening to my favourite song,
A lways miming along
P laying games I enjoy
T etris, a mentally challenging game
O ver-excitement at watching TV
P leased at cartoons, they're fun to me

I could eat chocolate every day,
But my mum won't let me have it that way.

I like snowflakes floating in the air,
Twinkling like crystals everywhere.

I like to play Monopoly,
It makes my sister, Kirsty, stroppy.

She always loses, I always win,
So I walk around with the biggest grin.

Leah Leonardi (9)

Me And My Friends

Me and my friends, we never fight,
We always make things alive and bright.
We chat together every day
And help chase life's blues away.
First there's Simran, then there's Izzy,
When put together they're always busy.
I can't forget Lizzie and Hannah,
For Lizzie's birthday we put up a banner.
Then there's the boys, all hard and rough,
Aaron, Harry, Alex and Bryn, they think they're really tough.
So that pretty much sums up my friends,
But I'm yet to tell you about the other twists and bends!

Bethan Evans (11)

MY FAVOURITE THINGS - Simply The Best

Wrestling

Wrestling is one of my favourite things,
The music, the wrestlers and the moves in the ring.
Do a move, like Batista,
Hasta la vista!
The man in the mask, Rey Mysterio,
Does the 619, ye ho!
Triple H says, 'Look at me!'
The Undertaker, he don't give a damn,
With his tombstone, last ride and choke slam.
Randy Orton with his RKO,
Takes out Chris Jericho.
I love Jeff Hardy, he is great,
With his 'whisper in the wind' and 'twist of fate .
The girls in the ring, they think they rule,
Mickie, Melina and Michelle McCool.
And then there's Kane, Tazz and Big Show,
Deuce, MVP and Carlitto.
I could go on, there's a whole load more,
In ECW, Smackdown and RAW!"
Awesome!

Ben Wilders (9)

My Favourite Things

All my best things -
Singing, dancing, making up different routines,
Whoo!

PlayStation, ice cream, sweets, chocolate,
My favourite things.

Acting strange, chatting, chillin' with friends,
Shopping,
All the best things!

X Factor, Britain's Got Talent, Big Brother
I'm A Celebrity, Get Me Out Of Here!

So they are my favourite things.

Kirsty Bishop (11)

Just A Few Things

Playing hockey and scoring goals,
Now here is where my favourite things unfold.
I'm just writing down a few of my favourite things,
From my pen to my paper no fibs, no strings.
Winter and Christmas and family cheer,
Family holidays and having fun,
Sitting by the pool, soaking up the sun,
Having a laugh, the fun never ends,
Getting dressed up for Hallowe'en,
Going out for us to be seen,
Watching TV on a Saturday night,
Strictly Come Dancing and X Factor's a delight,
On Easter day getting lots of chocolate eggs,
When my brother asks for a bit, no, but he still begs,
Having a hug and a kiss from my mum and dad,
Always lifts me up and stops me feeling sad,
Looking up at the stars in the night-time sky,
Watching the world pass on by.
This is a poem of my favourite things,
No fibs, no lies and no strings.

Victoria Evans (13)

I Like Lullabies

Hush, can you hear the thickening, deep in the air?
The trees are falling asleep.

Hush, can you see where the darkening skies
are stretched over the sunset?
Now close your heavy eyes.

Hush, can you hear where the whispering corn is settling down
And starting to yawn?

Hush, can you see in the moon's silver beam, the light of the world
Begging to dream?

Hush, can you feel the whole world sigh
And fall fast asleep to your best lullaby?

Nishath Jarin Pushpa (10)

MY FAVOURITE THINGS - Simply The Best

My Favourite Things

I like playing, in and out,
Jumping, skipping and shouting out,
I like playing in and out,
Singing, dancing and laughing out loud.
I like playing in and out,
Running, cycling, very, very fast.
I like playing in and out,
Writing, reading a very good book.
I like playing in and out,
Talking, chatting and being very cheeky.
I like playing in and out,
Paper, cardboard and lots of glue.
I like playing in and out,
Laughing, giggling on the trampoline.

Christmas, presents and treats,
Hallowe'en, trick or treat,
Lollies, chocolates of course,
Games, iPods and many more.

These are a few of my favourite things.

Jessica Gray (12)

Untitled

Girlie nights in with all your mates,
Chocolate bars and After Eights.
Takeaway pizza and sugary treats,
Ice cream and lots of sweets!

Happy Christmas nights,
Bright, warm fairy lights.
Fireworks and a bonfire,
Rockets rush higher and higher.

Crisp spring walks,
Flowers bloom from fragile stalks;
And autumn, a world of red and gold,
The changing days slowly getting cold.

Olivia Loizides (12)

My Favourite Things

Playing games on the laptop, in bed
Football with mates and the cat who gets fed.

Hiking in the countryside
And the horse which I ride,
Shopping in the biggest malls,
Watching the waterfalls.

Having snow fights,
Wearing green tights,
Ice skating in the rink,
Giving my boyfriend a wink!

Giving out Easter eggs
And shaving my hairy legs,
Having a dip in the swimming pool,
Hanging with friends, being cool.

Going to school and being taught,
On the way home to have thought.
Playing with dolls
And eating jam rolls.

Zainab Hussain (9)

The Bits And Bobs That Make Up Me!

Singing, dancing and prancing,
Having lots of fun and playing in the sun,
Making things with strings and wearing rings,
Splashing in water just like a sea otter,
Hanging out with friends while wearing new trends,
Sucking a tasty lollipop, while running away from the nasty cop,
Telling funny jokes and visiting old folks,
Taking part in a show and playing in the snow,
Smelling lovely flowers after taking twelve-hour showers,
Presents and treats, I can't wait to get sweets,
My teacher didn't mention that I had detention,
So I can rhyme any time that my teacher
Didn't mention that I had detention!

Samra Ibrar (8)

MY FAVOURITE THINGS - Simply The Best

What I Like Doing

Playing with animals, especially cats,
Riding too and kissing my mum and dad.
Playing my PlayStation and watching TV
And also eating and having tea.
Are some of these your favourite things?

Playing my violin and singing too,
Also dancing and playing Sims on my laptop.
Reading as well and playing with little kids,
My birthday as well,
Are some of these your favourite things?

Christmas and Hallowe'en and playing in the sun,
Don't forget about having fun.
Playing cards, especially spoons,
Are some of these your favourite things?

Playing with gadgets, playing chess,
Having parties, doing crafts
Going on holidays, reading too,
Are some of these your favourite things?

Jennifer Hornal (11)

Spring Birthday

This morning, looking out the window
I saw a squirrel running across the garden.
The bird singing a beautiful song,
The daffodil found a way to the light.
The flowers are blossoming.
The sun came out and I went out to play.
The wind blew me off my feet.
It's April, my favourite time of the year.

Spring is here,
Easter is here,
Birthday is here,
Cousins are here,
It's time to party.

Deborah Adewale (10)

My Favourite Things

M y favourite things, well, some of them anyway
Y ou are one them you know.

F avourite things, oh, let me think
A friend sleeping over is one of those things
V iolets are so nice, really nice
O h, let me think, what else?
U nique, we are, that's one of those things
R ebecca, my friend is one of them too
I like Christmas, my birthday yeah!
T he favourite thing I like most is playing with friends
E verything is maybe one of them

T wo more things I like are Easter, yum, yum and Hallowe'en, scary
H ello Kitty is the thing I love more than anything, except my family
I ce cream I really like, especially when I'm hot
N othing I don't like really, except five or six things
G reen grass is what I like in springtime, for the meantime
S ummertime is what I like, specially when I go on holidays

These are my favourite things.

Beth Coxon (10)

For The Love Of Christmas

Christmas time is a time of the year
When you forget all the troubles around the world
And enjoy the day of December 25th.

Now we have a credit crunch,
People are dying every day,
One thing in our heart
We couldn't forget this Christmas day,
The love of loved ones and the family around,
If you have no one you still have the memories
From when you were young.
Running down the stairs for Father Christmas
And opening up your presents,
That, you couldn't forget in this crazy world.

Asha Gilbert (11)

The Things I Love

My favourite thing is the blue of the sky,
The green of the grass.
The bird that sings beautiful songs,
In the tree at the bottom of my garden.

My favourite thing are my friends,
At school and home.
My family that protect me from harm,
They look after me wherever I go.

My favourite thing is to sit on my window sill
And look at the black of the night sky.
The moon that reflects the sun's light
And the bright, silver stars.

In short, I love nature,
Everything about it.
I also like birthdays and Christmas,
Ice cream and pizza,
But the best things I love are
Dancing and playing my flute.

Maria Walley (10)

These Are My Favourite Things

I love pushing Lego ships across a carpeted floor,
Reading of someone crossing a lonely moor,
So please, please give me some more!

Playing footy under a blazing sun,
Making snowmen and having great fun,
My mother giving me a hot cross bun.

Taking a photo of a ship's mast,
Playing a PS2 game where things move fast!
Trying to make a chocolate cake last.

Having guitar lessons, picking the notes,
Smelling the smell of baking cake as it floats,
Seeing the snow and putting on our coats.

Dusty Mason (10)

Christmas Poem

At Christmas I like
Getting up really early and tiptoeing around
Tip, tap, tip tap.

At Christmas I like
Ripping all the wrapping paper off my presents
Fisch, fisch!

At Christmas I like
Whizzing down snowy hills on my sledge
Whoosh, whoosh.

At Christmas I like
When the Christmas tree comes and gets brightly decorated.

At Christmas I like
Relatives coming around and putting lipstick marks on my face
Smooch, smooch.

At Christmas I like
A warm, tasty turkey dinner, with hot, thick gravy
I like Christmas!

Jack Barker (12)

An Angel Of Sadness

An angel I see in the sky,
Wings of pure white,
Shining hair and a smile on his face,
He has been seen before,
Maybe an old relative.
But all I see is the sadness in him
And the tears running out of his eyes.
Before he flies into the sunset
He gives me a look of bad news.
He is upset,
No one knows why,
But I have a feeling the angel
Was not meant to be dead.

Tamzin Stallard (10)

MY FAVOURITE THINGS - Simply The Best

My Favourite Things

Roses are red,
Violets are blue,
I like football,
Boxing too.
Racing cars,
Exploring stars.
Playing with friends
On electric guitars.
Listening to rock,
And eating a hock.
Watching Simpsons and Family Guy,
Jumping off walls, imagining I can fly.
Bowling a strike
And riding my bike.
Getting a wicket,
While playing cricket.
Going to school
To learn about Henry the king,
These are all my favourite things.

Rakim Sajero (10)

Untitled

PlayStation games and having some fun,
Getting some bananas, yum, yum, yum.

Smile to the camera at Christmas time,
Get some presents which are all mine, mine, mine.

Santa comes at Christmas, ho, ho, ho,
My favourite Simpson's character goes doh, doh, doh.

Balls, baubles, on the tree glistening at me,
Candy canes, just for me,
Happy families' laughing faces
Joy in all different places.

Different families, different,
We are grateful for God's good grace.

Alex Dougall (8)

Favourites

I like scoffing down chocolate, nothing better to eat,
To dance is to live, keep in time with the beat.
Cats are my favourite animals, so cuddly and cute,
Making music and singing and playing my flute.
Fave programme's Come Dancing, watch the pros do their prancing,
Liverpool - greatest team - they play like a dream.
I love slithering snakes, tarantulas too,
So fascinating to watch, my favourite colour is blue.
I love acting, I'm a real drama queen,
To do sport, cross-country, football and netball, I'm keen.
I collect gem-stones, they're sparkly and pretty,
I hang out with my mates and play with my kitty.
Tigers, cheetahs and monkeys, wild animals are cool,
I wish I could say the same about school.
Pressies on my birthday and at Christmas,
The latest cuddly toy with long kitten whiskers,
Listening to Black-Eyed Peas or Duffy sing,
If you like shopping then give me a ring.
These are a few of my favourite things.

Cara Mathews (12)

Charlie

Charlie is clever, comical and cool,
He's happy and he's smiley and he loves to go to school.
Adorable and loving, you get lost in his melting eyes.
Running here, there and everywhere,
He's playful, fun and bright.
Laughable and energetic,
He loves colours, sounds and lights.
Everyone thinks he's different, because he's handicapped,
But they're not right.
You'd be wrong if you thought that way,
He's the same as everyone,
He's number one,
And that's why we love him!

Rebecca Sheldon (11)

MY FAVOURITE THINGS - Simply The Best

My Favourite Things

These are some of my favourite things,
I like diamonds and rings,
The cute bird that sings,
Chocolate and toffee,
Milkshake and coffee,
Puppy dogs and butterflies,
Anything lovely I spot with my eyes.
The fluffy, bouncy bunny,
The bees smelling honey,
Animals and plants,
Elephants and ants,
Treetops and snowdrops,
Also the golden crops.
Girls Aloud,
Make a good sound,
They are my favourite band.
I love clothes and shoes,
Any kind will do,
Just as long as its one of my favourite things.

Ellis Martin (11)

Untitled

Diamonds and rubies are all shiny things.
Silver, gold, platinum, my favourite things!
Earrings, necklaces, bracelets and rings,
I do love jewellery, my favourite things!

Dairy Milk, Galaxy, Mars and Twix,
Oh so yummy, my favourite things.
Sunbites, Limbos, Snack-a-Jacks too,
Delicious crisps for me and you!

X Factor, Strictly and Big Brother too,
I love watching telly, that's all I do.
From singing to dancing to reality shows,
My favourite things are all of those.

Amber Walker (11)

A Bit O' This And A Bit O' That

There's a girl called Georgia, she's a real cool cat,
She likes a bit o' this and she likes a bit o' that.
Lush, creamy chocolate that melts in your mouth,
Deep crimson roses and birds flying south.
Glittery winter mornings, with layers of shimmering snow.
A crunch underfoot, wherever you go.
A bowl of vanilla ice cream and the whiskers on a cat.
Georgia likes a bit o' this and a bit o' that.
Christmas carols and ribbons, trees and twinkly lights.
Snuggly jumpers, gloves, scarves and hats,
And cold frosty nights.
Cuddles and kisses, relaxing with the family.
Reading for hours, curled up on the settee.
Listening to Rihanna or bands like Take That.
Georgia likes a bit o' this and a bit o' that.
Cutting and sticking, making birthday cards.
Paints and coloured pencils, making her mark!
There's a girl called Georgia, she's a super cool cat,
She likes a bit o' this and she likes a bit o' that.

Georgia Welch (12)

My Favourite Things

When I'm eating a bun,
I think it's lots of fun.
When I fly my kite,
It has a good height.

When my door goes *ding-dong,*
My friends come to play ping-pong.
When I play footie,
I put on my hoodie.

I like to box
When I'm wearing my socks.
These are the things I like,
Especially my brand new bike.

Carolina Valensise (9)

MY FAVOURITE THINGS - Simply The Best

Favourite Things

Some of my favourite things
Are chocolate, TV and rings.

I love playing on a golden beach,
Where green grass and cars seem out of reach.

I feel great when I shoot a hoop,
And climb up trees for abundant fruit.

Yummy strawberries and ice cream,
I really love playing on the netball team.

Reading, writing, playing in the snow,
So many places I love to go.

At Christmas putting tinsel on the tree,
In spring the handsome bumblebee.

Going to Sunday school
And playing pool.

Girl guides, roller coaster rides and cuddly toys,
But most of all, *lots of noise!*

Hannah Kelso-Mason (13)

Things I Like To Do

Watching TV is quite fun
And playing outside in the sun.
Cuddling my teddy when it's time for bed,
His trousers are green and his hat is red.

Computer games are really great
And playing cards with my mate.
Crosswords and puzzles blow my mind,
Clues and pieces not easy to find.

Getting messy with paint and pens,
Looking at insects through a lens.
Listening to music and eating sweets,
I am so lucky to have these treats.

Michelle Saunders (10)

My Favourite Things

My favourite things, I have so many,
Drinking Coke and eating jelly!
Going to the park, feeding ducks,
Watching films and reading books.
Taking walks, under the sun,
Running, skipping, simply having great fun!

Creating great things, both technical and arty,
Having special occasions, performances and parties.
Dancing on the dance floor, boogying all night,
Watching scary movies, which give you a fright!
Dressing in different ways, elegant, then funky.
Going out to Blackpool Zoo and watching swinging monkeys!

Travelling to Florida, riding great rides,
To feel the adrenaline rush go straight down my spine.
To feel the wind brush past my face,
As I race through the air at a terrific pace.
I love to sing and act and dance,
One of my life's dreams is to travel in France.

Hayley Hughes (11)

My Favourite Things

I love remote control cars and my favourite chocolate bar is Mars.
I read a variety of books and enjoy dressing up as Captain Hook.
My favourite sport is cricket,
I always play it when it is sunny.
When it's bedtime I love my hot drink with honey.

I like riding on my bike
And then having a session of beat boxing on my mike.
Birthdays and cakes are my favourite things too,
I also enjoy mending my broken toys with glue.

The best thing of all is when I accomplish missions
on my Nintendo Wii,
I could play all day, while Mum sits drinking a cup of tea.

Keshav Bhardwaj (10)

My Favourite Things

Going to dancing and cuddling pets,
Hanging around, shooting balls in the net!
Kisses from brother, hugs from mum,
Going to school and doing my sums.

Watching The X Factor, reading a book,
Hanging with friends, attempting to cook!
Playing on DS, sitting in the sun,
Families and holidays, having fun.

Birthdays and Christmas presents and joy,
Family spirit, family love, giving them the perfect toy!
Listening to music, going on the computer,
Looking at pugs, that will never get any cuter.

Making cards and playing a game,
Stroking my pet, Stripe, that is her name!
Eating ice cream and buying sweets,
Painting my toenails on my feet!

These are my favourite things!

Chloe Roberts (12)

My Favourite Things

Fizzy pop and cheese.
I hate these,
But I love some of these,
Mammy, Daddy and a big, fat kiss
And writing my Christmas list.

Reading, writing and lots, lots more,
Let's see what teachers have in store.
Arts and crafts and making a card,
All of this doesn't seem hard.

So now you have heard my rhyme,
It is my bed time,
I would like to tell you before mum gets cross
That my name is Hannah Voss!

Hannah Voss (11)

My Favourite Things

I love my cakes,
So warm when they're baked.

I love my bed,
Along with my ted.

These are a few of my favourite things.

I love my hair,
So shiny and fair.

I love to cook,
As long as I have a cooking book.

These are a few of my favourite things.

I love the snow,
But it always seems to go.

I love my mum,
She's so fun.

These are a few of my favourite things.

Rosie Reville (10)

Farm Houses

Don't be a litter lout
And throw your rubbish about.

Always throw your bottle or tin
In the rubbish bin.

Another thing farmer hates,
If you don't shut the gate.

Because his animals will stray
And some run away.

Keep your dog on a lead,
Or it may chase the sheep and make them bleed.

If the farmer sees it, he may shoot it,
Because trespassers will be prosecuted.

Hasnain Ali (10)

MY FAVOURITE THINGS - Simply The Best

Sweets,

Sweets, sweets, stupendous sweets,
Chocolate and humbugs,
Toffees and chewing gum,
Sweets, sweets,
So many to name.

Sweets are delicious,
Bucketsful of happiness
A lovely treat
To satisfy your taste-buds.

Sweets are like awards,
A lovely prize to win
Sweets are the cure
For an everlasting bore.

Colas and sherbets
Liquorice and taste-busters
Sweets, sweets,
So many to name.

Louise Jesi (11)

My Dog, Dilly

She is white
And never does bite,
She would win first place
In a best dog race.
She is blessed with a kindly heart,
Nothing could draw me and Dilly apart.
She is six years old
And though bold, does what she's told.
She's not the tallest dog that I've met,
But neither the smallest - I bet.
She is a soppy Labrador
And better than all the rest - I'm sure.
There couldn't be a better dog than Dilly,
   . . . so saying yours is better is just silly!

Cressi Sowerbutts (11)

My Personality

When I'm asleep at night in my bed
With crazy dreams
Dancing through my head,
I think of my favourite things,
Dancing, prancing and a little sing.

When you see those actresses on TV
Doing drama just like me,
Ballet, tap and modern too,
All the things I like to do.

I cook at home, I cook at school,
I think cooking's really cool.
My favourite day of the year
Is Christmas with that jolly cheer.

Shopping is my hobby too,
Some more things I like to do.
All these things are part of me
And maybe what I'd like to be.

Nicole Roberts (Batty) (12)

Day By Day

My best thing is going to school
And not to be a fool.
Learn my lessons the easy way
And not to copy the person on that day.
Homework is a bit of a blow,
Sometimes I am a bit slow.
Done my homework for the week,
I do not know what the teacher thinks.
Hark, the birds are singing in the tree,
I have counted two or three.
A blackbird and two robin redbreasts out there,
The branch of a tree looks a bit bare,
The birds have flown away,
They will be back another day.

Sophie Mallen (11)

MY FAVOURITE THINGS - Simply The Best

Christmas

Christmas, Christmas, is so much fun,
The best time of the year.
Opening presents under the Christmas tree,
Waiting, waiting, what will it be?
An XBox 360, PSP, £5.00 and a Nintendo Wii,
Whoopee!

But I wonder who sent these?
Was it Mum or was it Dad?
Or was it my auntie and uncle?
Oh please, please can you tell me?

Father Christmas of course, AKA Santa Claus,
He was the one who sent all these things,
You know I knew it all along,
I was just testing you!

My favourite thing is
Christmas,
Is it yours too?

Klara Prela (9)

What I Like Best Of All

Watching TV,
Being cheeky,
Playing robbers and cops,
Playing on laptops,
Camping with the boys,
Playing with my toys,
Making loads of noise
And counting my coins,
Blowing in my trumpet,
Eating lots of crumpet,
Burying all my dead pets,
Digging in the sand,
Making my own band
And holding, hand in hand.

Robin Hannay (8)

My Favourite Things

Going to the zoo and swimming too,
These are two things I love to do.

Seeing my next-door neighbour's dog
Hiding in the trees,
He is such a joy to me
And he's something I love to see.

Summer flowers, so bright and sweet,
As I sit in the garden with my ice cream to eat.

Watching TV, snuggled up in bed,
Just resting my dozy little head,
Not forgetting my cuddly ted.

Easter Sunday with chocolate eggs,
A birthday party with all my friends.
Christmas time with trees and lights,
Lots of chocolate and Turkish delight.

Mmmm, my favourite things.

Alison McAliece (9)

My Favourite Things

From fashion to food
And being in a good mood,
A Christmas treat
Or a bag of chocolate and sweets.
A diamond or two,
And a pair of Gucci shoes.
The many things life brings
Are just a few of my favourite things.

Make-up and phones,
Along with ice cream in cones.
My best friends and more,
What else could I ask for?
These many things life brings
Are all my favourite things!

Keshini Gooneratne (14)

MY FAVOURITE THINGS - Simply The Best

What I Like Best

I like playing on the PlayStation,
Sword fighting, adventure and shooting.
I like robots, I can dance and talk like them
And you tell them what to do.

That's what I like.

I like doing karate, I am enjoying it,
I like tournaments the most.
I like swimming, it's really fun,
The best part is splashing the water.

That's what I like.

What I like is so cool,
I'm so big I don't need a stool.
But what I like most of all are animals,
And my whole family, my mum and bro.

That's what I like.
That's what I like most of all.

Charles Gibbons (11)

My Favourite Things

Hearing Girls Aloud and McFly sing,
Loving them dance and sing,
While playing with my pet on the floor,
Next day going to school and learning things.
After school, playing on my game,
Laughing happily and watching the screen,
Going to bed and having a good night's sleep,
Waking up and having my breakfast
With my brother, having my Advent calendar,
Playing in the sun and having a drink,
On the step, smiling all day long,
Hearing the ice cream man calling my mum,
My mum saying yes, running out of the door,
Eating my ice cream, laughing back to the house.

Chelsea Kelly (8)

My Favourite Things

One of my favourite things is football,
I love football and I love playing it in the rain.
I also love creamy, delicious chocolate,
It's so nice and yummy,
Especially when it reaches my tummy!
I love lots of food, like curry,
Ice cream, roast and chilli,
But if I eat too much,
It makes me silly.
But my favourite thing I've ever done
Is to go to Spain on a big aeroplane,
It was the best thing ever.
Swimming in the pool or sea,
It tastes so salty just for me.
My uncle's boat was such fun,
We went really fast, we went so fast
It was like we were going to the past.
These are the most favourite things in my life.

Luke Dawes (11)

My Favourite Things

The colourful sky of fiery amber, as the sun goes away
The daring, black clouds of rain, haunting every day
The oceans delicate waves, swirling turquoise and blue
The twinkling stars at midnight, watching over you
The eerie, silver moon, glowing softly white
The pouring afternoon rain, which umbrellas fight
The looming, towering trees, they stand in autumn red
The many muddy lakes, in which ducks are fed
The lush and healthy mountains, beautifully fresh and green
The crispy, icy snow, in the cold winter seen
The children in playgrounds, shrieking, high-pitched and shrill
The weak wind blowing calmly against an old windmill
The things that are favoured, happily, by me
May seem quite simple but at least they're completely free!

Hannah Clifford (11)

MY FAVOURITE THINGS - Simply The Best

My Favourite Things

M y favourite things are very important
Y ours might be the same as mine

F un things for you to do
A re already there for me and you
V arieties of holidays, parties and treats
O ur place is full of feasts
U nwrapping presents for Christmas and New Year
R ecreating the decorations every year
I ce and icicles make the winter look pretty
T asting yummy Indian dates
E ating delicious chocolate cakes

T ea parties for your mates and friends
H earing the chimes of Big Ben
I ncredible books with interesting bits
N utritious fruits will keep you fit
G etting your favourite book at least
S eeing the sun rise in the east.

Athnah Justus (10)

My Favourite Things

Meatballs and rice in a big, round pot,
Goes in my tummy and hits the spot.
Singing and dancing, I love to do,
It helps me a lot if I'm feeling blue.
I love all animals, that you can bet,
When I grow up I'll be a vet.
My mum is fab, she's a very good cook,
Whatever I do she wishes me luck.
My dad is so cool and his name is Mike,
He buys me lots of things I like.
I have two pets, one likes a jog,
Sausage the hamster and Kane the dog.
Thank you for listening to my favourite things,
I almost forgot . . . I love chicken wings!

Paige James (10)

Coral Reefs

I'm swimming, swimming through the wide, open seabeds of the oceans of Australia, where the tropical fishes are gliding across the coral reefs.

The spongy seabeds are surrounded by
groups of different fish species,
The fish I see are having lots of fun.
Little fishes are chasing round each other, round and round.
There are also jellyfish nearby, swimming up and down.

I like to take photos of what I see down here,
I take them with my memory,
Not all the time.
When the light shines on the fishes,
Their stripes glow like rich jewels of topaz and silver.
I'm a diver,
I love taking photos of the things I've talked about.
These are my favourite things.
Are they yours?

Anisa Zahid Fazil (11)

The Things That Matter To Me

Singing to McFly or cheering for Liverpool,
Listening to my music or winning at baseball,
Flying to Las Vegas or watching great TV,
These are the things that matter to me.

Eating lots of ice cream or listening to the rain,
Reading a good book again and again,
Stroking my pet cat or climbing a tree,
These are the things that matter to me.

Opening presents and parcels, or playing a game of football,
Messing around with my mobile and driving my mum up the wall,
Hearing the roar of a tiger, or playing on a Wii,
These are the things that matter to me.

 Bethan Wood (10)

MY FAVOURITE THINGS - Simply The Best

My Favourite Things

These are a few of my favourite things!
I get goosebumps when the X Factor finalists sing,
I love the X Factor.
I love seeing Manchester United score a goal,
I love Manchester United.
Heat magazine and the latest celeb gossip,
Reading Heath with a Galaxy chocolate bar.

Shopping, ice skating, watching TV,
The luxury days with my laptop on my knee,
Top nosh at Christmas time, as well as birthdays,
And I can't resist cute, furry animals.

Hoodies and Ugg boots - such comfy clothes,
Music and holidays,
Getting a suntan in summer,
Prawn cocktail crisps are always on my list
When my mum goes shopping.
Those were a few of my favourite things!

Chloe Warburton (10)

Things I Love

I love, opening presents and eating Christmas dinner,
Then curling up nice and cosy in front of the warm, open fire,
Where I dream of going to the beach with my bucket and spade,
Warm, summer days and eating ice cream in the shade.

I love red, purple, blue and green,
These are the colours of the rainbows I have seen.
Eating sweets and staying up late,
Then have sleepovers with my best mates.

I love cold, frosty mornings,
So I can watch my breath dancing in the air.
Bonfire night parties
And Christmas carols in the square.

Georgia Walther (8)

Pastimes, Hobbies, Interests, Faves

I like the computer,
I like all the games,
I'd like to play them every day!

Crisps, chocolate and sweets,
I'd like every day to be a treat!
I like all the bubbles in fizzy pop,
But I don't like when my ice cream goes plop and drops.

I like playing with my friends,
Till the day ends.
I feel so free playing with others
And not just me!

Books are the best,
Books are my faves,
I read one or two once a day.

These are my favourite things
I wouldn't want to change a thing!

Cassandra Boyce (11)

Fabulous Friends

My favourite things are friends,
They're pretty great to have.
They're quite a blessing to us,
Which we must clearly love.

And if we make a good friend,
They will really pick you up.
The bond will always be so special,
Great mates are really tops.

Because my friends to me are . . .
The icing on my cake, the glitter in my eyes,
The moat around my castle, the success in all my tries,
The top inside my hat, the sole that's in my shoe,
So next time you see your friends, shout
'I love you!'

Amy Clarke (13)

MY FAVOURITE THINGS - Simply The Best

My Favourite Things

J.R.R. Tolkien and Agatha Christie,
Days when it's snowy and frosty and misty.
Grey dolphins jumping, as if they had wings.
These are a few of my favourite things.

Tropical waters and glistening beaches,
Eating ice cream with round, amber peaches,
Christmas and sparkle and crackers with rings,
These are a few of my favourite things.

Writing and drawing and puzzles and quizzes,
Fresh lemonade that bubbles and fizzes,
School Christmas Concerts and the carols we sing,
These are a few of my favourite things.

Finally, this poem has come to an end,
But my favourite thing is surely a friend,
What else brings all of the joy a friend brings,
And that is why they are my favourite things.

Anusia Battersby (11)

I Like . . .

My bedroom with pink things
My necklaces and big rings
My books and my mobile
To text all my friends.

My brothers, just sometimes
My food when it's teatime
My after school clubs
Where I meet all my friends.

My parents and Granny, my aunties Lindsey and Manni
Grandad and uncles
They all make good friends.

I like all my friends
They are the best things
Nobody else makes me laugh, play and sing.

Ailsa Knight (9)

Untitled

When I am down, feel rather glum,
My favourite thing is a hug from my mum.
When I am lonely, when nobody's there,
A hug from my mum rips away my despair.

Whenever the sun doesn't shine on my face,
Or a friend isn't there to care or embrace,
When my friends move away, when they have all gone,
My mum offers her shoulder which I cry on.

I love my mummy and she loves me
And if me and mum ever disagree
We make up in a blink of an eye
And cuddle together, till the sun has passed by.

So, in conclusion, my favourite thing
Is not to dance, read or sing,
But to cuddle my mother and give her my heart
And give love to each other till we have to part.

Abigail Swift (12)

My Favourite Things

Sleeping in late,
Cuddling my cat,
Watching Brad Pitt . . . and dreaming
Of my favourite things.

The colour pink,
My music,
Looking out of the window . . . and dreaming
Of my favourite things.

Reading adventure stories,
Watching tigers on TV,
Raindrops . . . and dreaming
Of my favourite things.

Going to sleep . . . and dreaming
About tomorrow.

Jade Armer (14)

MY FAVOURITE THINGS - Simply The Best

My Favourite Things

Dancing and singing is really, really fun,
Going to the bakers to get an iced bun.
Reading and writing is all I like to do,
Running to the shops to get a pair of shoes.
Holidays to islands in the sun,
Jamaica and Barbados, they're the best ones.

My favourite pet is my little tabby cat,
He is very furry, but he's not very fat.
Playing on consoles and having treats,
Lying on the sofa, sneaking little sweets.
Going to swimming pools in the summer times,
Looking at lemons and looking at limes.

I'd like to win the laptop so I can write lots of things
And have a smile on my face with the joy it brings!

I hope you like my poem, I really thought it through,
Have a very merry Christmas and Happy New Year too!

Aaliyah Jordan (11)

Annoying Things

I like to play on the swings,
Do lots of things, including my Nintendo Wii
And buy games that I see.

Drive my dad mad,
Act like a lad,
Pick all the daisies.

Still play with my Bratz
And chase after cars all day long.

There's lots of things about me you see.

I play with cuddly toys,
Hang out with the boys,
Sing a song to my mother.

And that's it for now.

Holly Griffiths (10)

My Favourite Things

I like rugby, tennis
And football too.
Tae-kwon-do and swimming,
So much to do.

I also love animals,
Both big and small,
From dogs down to gerbils,
I just love them all.

My friends are important,
See them at school,
They're there when I need them,
They are so cool.

And last but not least,
My whole family,
They always support me,
That's how it should be!

Rachel Hollingworth (10)

My Favourite Things

I like music, chocolates and treats,
That includes eating lots of sweets.

Going to school and learning DT,
Design Technology,
Is the subject for me.

Opening presents, surprises to come,
I love getting kisses from my dad and my mum.

Watching TV and reading a book,
Eating ice cream and creating weird stuff.

Going on safari or maybe to the zoo,
Play on the computer, win a game or two.

Pulling funny faces, jumping up and down,
Riding on my bicycle, smile, but never a frown.

Josephine Ruiz (10)

MY FAVOURITE THINGS - Simply The Best

My Favourite Things

Play-fighting with brothers,
Having fun with friends,
Watching High School Musical
And cycling round the bends.

Making paper origami,
Listening to Girls Aloud,
Their music makes me want to dance,
Their parents must be proud.

Going out and playing with the neighbours
And making them smile,
Teaching them how to ride their bikes,
But that just takes a while.

Reading my book,
Being quite tall,
But Young Writers poetry,
I love you all.

Sophie Cook (11)

My Favourite Things

Chocolate, sweets and parties too,
Visiting friends and X Factor, don't you?

I love Christmas and Easter, those days are the best
So much better than the rest

Swimming and dancing are my favourite sports
They are sometimes included in my thoughts

My birthday is a special day
I always wake up and shout hooray

I love my soft pillow, where I rest my head
When I'm in my cosy bed

My favourite teddy is my Build-a-Bear
I bought some clothes for it to wear
And these are a few of my favourite things.

Katy Hodgson (10)

Down On The Beach

Down on the beach
Playing in the sand,
Lazing in the sun
And getting very tanned.

Down on the beach
Splashing in the sea,
'Hey,' little fishes
Come and play with me.

Down on the beach
Eating ice cream,
Sprinkles on the top,
Oh what a dream.

Down on the beach
The sun begins to set,
Time to go home now,
It's been a day I won't forget.

Maisie Wilders (7)

My Favourite Things

My favourite things are glorious things,
That grow inside my brain.
They wiggle and squiggle around in my head,
How could it ever be plain?

There are
Stories and bugs,
Warm, great, big hugs,
Jigsaws and writing and flowers!
Monsters and planes,
Long country lanes,
Game consoles,
Fighting with powers!

My favourite things are glorious things,
Nothing can ever divide us!

Siobhan Bailey (9)

My Favourite Things

Riding my bike,
Playing in the park,
Watching the stars
In the sky after dark.

Eating ice lollies,
Licking ice cream,
Going to bed
And having a nice dream.

Reading a book,
Watching TV,
Making my mum
A nice cup of tea.

Can't wait 'til Christmas,
When it's twenty more sleeps.
Fun, glee and laughter,
Presents and treats.

Alicia Jones (9)

My Favourite Things

Cars and motorcycles,
Whilst out on my bike,
XBox or PlayStation,
When it's wet outside.

History or engineering,
Whilst I'm sat at school,
On the weekend
I enjoy jumping into the pool.

Football on Saturday,
Scoring lots of goals,
Training on Tuesdays,
Improving our skills on the ball.

Jack King (14)

My Favourite Things

I like rabbits, spiders and pigs,
Cats, rats and anything that digs,
Christmas gives me a set of wings,
These are a few of my favourite things.

Watching TV, books, games and videos,
Listening to my favourite music on stereos,
If I see a grasshopper I give it a few pings,
These are a few of my favourite things.

Computer games, gadgets and playing football,
Spending money at the shopping mall,
Jewellery and motorbikes, a noise that dings,
These are a few of my favourite things.

Singing and dancing to a good song,
Doing something bad and hit on the head with a dong,
Laughing when Akon or 30 Seconds to Mars sings,
These are a few of my favourite things.

Steven Baird (10)

My Favourite Things

Seeing my dogs' excited faces,
Playing the guitar, knowing the basics.
Listening to Eminem and 50 Cent,
Calzaghe boxing, what a gent.

Playing on my Wii,
Dipping biscuits in my tea,
Playing with my older brothers,
Chatting to my cousins.

Reading Catherine Fisher's books,
Not caring how I look.
Sleeping late every weekend,
Now this poem is at an end.

Rachael Pippen (14)

MY FAVOURITE THINGS - Simply The Best

My Weekend!

Nice lay in, snuggled up in my bed,
Then get up, get dressed and get this weekend started!
Rockin' out to tunes on the stereo,
Turning up the music as loud as it can go!

Playing on my laptop, then shop for a dress,
Get the make-up and some shoes, got to be the best!
The handbag, nails and more!
Gonna be shopping for hours, maybe four!

Next day, play footie with my brother and dad,
It turns out I'm not that bad.
Watching TV whilst eating treats,
Because I just love my sweets!

Now it's party time, get ready, let's go,
Texting my friends to let them know.
We're here! Let's dance, scoff down sweets, drink pop!
I wish the weekend would never stop!

Grace Mitchell (13)

My Favourite Things

Some of my favourite things are
Swimming in the pool and relaxing in the spa,
Birthday parties and water fights,
Summer holidays and flying kites.

Shopping in Leeds and watching TV,
Playing in the garden and on the Nintendo Wii,
Roller coasters and swimming in the lake,
Cross-country races and baking a cake.

Roller skating down the street,
Out on Hallowe'en with a bag full of sweets,
Wrapping presents and Christmas cheer,
Christmas is my favourite time of year!

Hannah Brown (13)

These Are My Favourite Things

Painting winter pictures
Dancing at school discos
Chilling with my friends
These are my favourite things.

Surfing on the computer
Watching scary movies
Reading Harry Potter
These are my favourite things.

Playing with my cat
Eating melted chocolate
Camping with my friends
These are my favourite things.

Sunbathing when on holiday
Unwrapping Christmas presents
Listening to my music
These are my favourite things.

Anne Dillon (13)

My Rocking Horse

Through the woods,
Duck under the branch,
Jump over the stream,
I can see the ranch.

Cross over the road,
Change the gait to trot,
Go straight into canter,
Though it's getting too hot.

I hear my mum shouting,
I must finish this course
And return another day
To my great rocking horse!

Bethany Hinds (12)

MY FAVOURITE THINGS - Simply The Best

These Are A Few Of My Favourite Things

I like eating little iced buns,
Going shopping for shoes and little toy guns,
Meeting my friends with all their mums,
These are a few of my favourite things!

I like PlayStations, books and big bear hugs,
When I get happy I buy fluffy rugs,
I have my own decorative mugs,
These are a few of my favourite things!

I like lollipops and little sweets,
Sugary doughnuts and special treats,
Those little jellybeans and those paper sheets,
These are a few of my favourite things!

I like playing, especially cards,
Skipping and dancing and a game of charades,
Going out to have a game of darts,
These are a few of my favourite things!

Tyler Booker (12)

My Favourite Things 2008

Laptops and gadgets, playing with my pets
Playing in the garden happily, having fun.
Playing in my room all day long,
Visiting my friends every day.
These are a few of my favourite things.

Having a bath, relaxing in the sun,
Playing in the pool, having great fun,
Drama, science, maths and lots more.
These are a few of my favourite things.

DS, PlayStations, games and lots more,
Dancing and disco.
These are a few of my favourite things.

Aimee Davies (10)

Wonderful Worlds

Reading great books that I can't put down.
They always make sure that I don't wear a frown.
Lost in a world where no one can find me,
But my faithful book characters will always stick by me.

Drawing designs for a great fashion show.
Just pick up a pencil and off I will go.
Dresses and skirts, T-shirts and boots tied with laces
And making my models wear funny faces!

Hearing rock music or playing my cello,
The sound is so deep and yet it is mellow.
Creating such a wonderful atmosphere,
Both are favourite sounds to hear.

Meeting animals at a country farm,
They turn to see me then switch on their charm.
Riding a horse and hearing birds sing,
These are a few of my favourite things.

Emma Williams (11)

Tiger The Pussy Cat

Once upon a time, in a place called Carryduff,
There was a little cat who was feeling a bit rough.
Now, he knew of a nice house in Marlborough Park,
So he went and miaowed, well, he couldn't bark.
When the door was opened, inside he went,
Oh how nice and warm, so he felt content.
The family seemed nice and really quite good,
So he miaowed again, because he wanted some food.
They gave him some milk, then made a wee bed,
He felt nice and cosy and now he was fed.
The pussy cat felt he had landed quite well,
So now he walks tall and he's looking quite swell.

Deborah Mills (11)

MY FAVOURITE THINGS - Simply The Best

Untitled

Ozzy, Ozzy, you are cool,
And also you are small.
You're a brindle, you're bright,
And you will always cause a fight.

On the bunk-bed you will jump,
On the bed there is a lump,
You are always in the house,
Keeping quiet like a mouse.

You are always on your feet,
Whilst you eat your dog treat,
All the food that I don't eat,
You seem to always get the meat.

When we take you to the park,
You see your friends and start to bark,
Ozzy, Ozzy, you're my friend
And friendship never ends.

Trevor Tooth (11)

My Favourite Things

I love the feeling when Friday is here
And the chance to relax is finally near
Time in my room with a book or my knights
Will there be victory for the reds, greens or whites?
Saturday morning and no clock by my head
I can play with my DS while I lie in my bed
My cat's come upstairs to sleep in my room
I can stay in my PJs - sometimes till noon
Sunday arrives and the chance of a swim
Or a game of badminton, which I usually win!
I then play the piano or beat my score on the Wii
Then the weekend is over and it's school now for me.

Charles Woolhouse (11)

Cool Cars

Cool cars are fast
Some are slow
If you don't believe me
Ask your Auntie Moe.

Faster than the speed of light
The seat belts are really light
Leather seats
And rapping beats.

Fifteen inch plasma
Behind the front seat
Hydraulics and nitros
Booming like a treat.

They never look tatty
Even with a flatty
Engines roar
While playing hardcore.

Curtis Hannington (10)

Summer

Looking at the sun
Having some fun
Playing in the pool
Trying to keep cool
Having some sweets
And lots of treats
Lying in the sun
Cuddling my mum
Going down the slide
Swimming side by side
Waiting to be fed
It is time for bed.

Chantal Kaufman (11)

MY FAVOURITE THINGS - Simply The Best

Sailing

I push the boat out,
Put the dagger board in,
Let out the sail,
Away I go.

The boat is bobbing,
The sail ripples,
I pull it in,
Away, away, I go.

The wind picks up,
It catches the sail,
I shoot forward,
Away, away, away, I go.

In the distance is the shore,
That is where I am heading,
That is where I stop,
Back, back, back, I go.

William Shepherd (10)

Lots Of My Favourite Things

I have a lot of favourite things,
I really don't know where to begin!
Maybe it's dancing to Girls Aloud,
Or singing Christmas songs at school, makes me feel proud.
I love EastEnders, it's really good,
I would star in it, if I could.
Sleepovers are really cool,
With all my best friends from my school.
I also love parties and bowling too
And going on holiday, how about you?
But best of all, it has to be,
Hugging my family, who really love me!

Eleanor Morgan (10)

Christmastime Again

It wasn't all that long ago,
Before Christmas was here,
But now it's back again,
The lights, trees and cheers.

Even though I get a lot of presents,
From those who are very dear,
Some people, all over the world
Are sitting, shedding a tear.

All the food lay on the table,
Ready for us to eat,
Lots of different types to chose from,
Vegetables, potatoes and meat.

Every lovely decoration,
Mum's out up with me.
We all help to set the table
While Dad prepares the tea.

Vanessa Nakitende (11)

Santa Claus Is So Special

I love the snow,
That makes things glow.
Santa Claus is so special.
I love snowflakes,
That love to snow shake.
Santa Claus is so special.
I love presents
From my parents.
Santa Claus is so special.
I love snowmen,
Hiding in the snow den.
Santa Claus is so special!

Tiegan Flynn (10)

Fresh Air

I like to play outside,
It could be in the garden,
I don't really care where,
I just love the fresh air.

With my ball
Or on my bike,
I even like
To fly my kite.

When it's wet and cold outside,
You will hear me say,
Wet, wet, rain, go away,
Or I cannot come out to play.

I ask my mum, 'What can I do today?
I cannot go out to play.'
'Never mind,' she would say,
'Tomorrow is another day.'

Karsha Brown (10)

My Favourite Things

Horse riding and birthdays,
Opening up presents,
Looking at birds, like cockerels and pheasants.
Chatting to friends and learning at school,
Dancing to music at parties is cool.

Chocolate spread sandwiches are delicious to eat,
Chinese on Saturdays is always a treat.

Now it is time for my most favourite of all,
A white Bengal tiger, with cubs so small,
So fluffy and white and really cute,
First day of birth, really minute.

Emily Price (10)

My Favourite Things

Decorating cakes with icing and sweets
Birthday parties and surprising treats
Painting butterflies' colourful wings
These are some of my favourite things.

Going on a water slide and skipping with a rope
Building a sleigh as slippery as soap
Eating lots of chocolate Easter eggs in spring
These are some of my favourite things.

Reading books all day long
Watching TV or listening to a song
Blowing up balloons as round as rings
These are some of my favourite things.

Going outside to play in the snow
Playing Ludo and Four In A Row
Being inventive with cardboard and string
These are all of my favourite things.

Sabina Saleem (11)

Summer Holidays

Nintendo DS and playing in the sun,
Playing with my friends and having lots of fun.

Riding on my bicycle, watching out for trees,
Chatting and talking, watching out for bees.

I love to bake; sweets and treats and things to eat,
Cake, biscuits I *love* to eat!

I love to create a lot of things,
Posters, flyers, colourful things.

Fun days are over, they were so cool,
Now it's time to go back to school.

Zulaikah Patel (11)

MY FAVOURITE THINGS - Simply The Best

My Favourite Things

My favourite things are . . .
Running to the horizon where the sun sets.
Competing for the record which is best.
Don't worry because I will be there in a spin.
But these are a few of my favourite things.

Dancing the night away to the beat,
Next day your friends are off to the Ukraine.
Playing basketball is my favourite sport,
I like it when you dribble it up and down the court.
These are a few of my favourite things.

Playing PS3 and Nintendo Wii,
Eating my freshly grown peas.
These are a few of my favourite things.

Playing hide and seek, exploring the trees,
If we were able to play, would you find me?
These are a few of my favourite things.

Kaelan Wade (12)

My Favourite Things!

Eating strawberry sweets and skipping in spring,
These are a few of my favourite things.

Reading a book about queens and kings,
This is another of my favourite things.

Colouring in and doing drawings,
These are more of my favourite things.

Listening to Girls Aloud sing,
This is one of my favourite things.

Having a party or playing on swings,
These are all of my favourite things!

Chloe Murray (10)

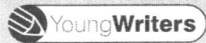

Down At The Bowling Alley

Down at the bowling alley,
Waiting for your turn,
Thinking what to do next,
You look and then you learn.

Then finally that time comes
When no one else matters,
Just hit it down the middle
And strike the rest to tatters.

Then you get that feeling
That lifts you in the air,
That time that is so special,
When everyone should care.

'Cause it's that time of day, that time of life,
That makes you feel the best,
That makes you feel so special,
Better than the rest!

Molly Burford (12)

Holidays

I like holidays,
Playing in the sun
I like holidays,
They are fun
I like holidays,
Visiting different countries
I like holidays,
Speaking 1,000 languages
I like holidays,
Laying in the beach
I like holidays,
Playing in the sun!

Wendy Su (12)

MY FAVOURITE THINGS - Simply The Best

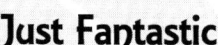

Just Fantastic

Riding a bike and playing a game,
Camping in the forest and hiking in the mountains,
Riding a horse and going around the world,
Are some of my favourite things I like to perform.

Playing with my pet and giving it a scrub,
Inventing something new and having some fun,
Collecting stamps and reading a good book,
Are some of my favourite things I like to do.

Dressing up as an astronaut and acting like one,
Collecting gadgets and monitoring them,
Eating ice cream and buying chocolates
Are some of my favourite things I like to do.

Going to the beach and making castles,
Going to school and gaining knowledge,
Playing badminton and scoring a goal
Are some of my favourite things I like to perform.

Sanka Edirisinghe (11)

Girls In The World

Girls, girls, girls,
The best in the world,
All they do is play with pearls.

Super girls, super girls,
They're truly the best,
All they fiddle with is their big, puffy curls.

Girly girls and tomboys,
Different on the outside,
But all play with toys.

Rebecca Pendry (10)

Favourite Things

PlayStation games and things to eat,
That's what I call a really good treat.
Sometimes I mess with wedding rings,
These are some of my favourite things.

I just love to play in the sun,
While it's hot I'll have great fun.
When I'm bored I start to sing,
These are some of my favourite things.

When it rains, it's really lame,
But that same day a friend came.
We started playing queens and kings,
These are some of my favourite things.

Now I have to say goodnight,
The time I've had has been real bright.
I just love to eat hot wings,
These are some of my favourite things.

Remel Enyioko-Bakers (12)

My Favourite Things

Drawing, painting, arts and crafts,
Going to stay little and building rafts.
These are just some of my favourite things.

Reading, singing and climbing trees too,
I'd be up a tree all day, with my crew,
These are just some of my favourite things.

Netball, football and computers,
I'm so good at these, I don't need any tutors.
These are just some of my favourite things.

Lara Howells (10)

MY FAVOURITE THINGS - Simply The Best

Are These Any Of Your Fave Things?

Playing on the Wii, fajitas for tea,
Movies and snowmen, writing with my pen,
Spiderwick stories about fairies and things,
Now that's just a few of my favourite things!
Living in Wales, sleeping tops 'n' tails,
Singing and dancing, hopping and prancing,
Rapping to a song sung by the Ting Tings,
These are more of my favourite things.
Toffee Crisps, tasty - yum yum!
Lots of them going in my tum.
It's winter now, summer has gone,
The cold breezy nights drone on and on.
It's fun with the family though, even the dog,
Although she is a bit of a fire-hog!
Forever and ever I'll love to write
And all these things I have written now
Will be cherished in my heart somehow.

Emily Jones (12)

The Best

My favourite thing is the best for me,
I always have to look and see.
I think it's really great,
But sometimes I get late.
For school of course
And sometimes for my chores.

But never mind that,
My sister just sat
On my book,
Why does she always look
When I am hiding it?
Then she takes it,
I shout at her and tell her to stop it
And what does she say?
Nothing, just walks away!

Thaniya Miah (12)

My Favourite Things

M y cherry-red home-made stunt kite
Y orkshire puddings, fluffy and light

F unny faces and silly looks
A drian Mole, my favourite books
V ictory for my favourite team
O r a clear blue drinkable stream
R acing games on my PS3
I 'd love to get a Nintendo Wii
T alking to my mates on MSN
E ven my best friend, good old Ben

T rees swaying in the warm breeze
H olidays near all the seven seas
I saac, my spotted white dog
N othing but a Christmas Yule log
G olf is my favourite sport
S quid that is freshly caught.

Wayne Perks (13)

Happiness

Happiness sounds like people having lots of fun,
Happiness feels like the blazing sun,
Happiness smells like sweet honey,
Happiness looks like lots of money,
Happiness tastes like orange juice,
Happiness is sleeping moose.

Happiness is my favourite thing because
It makes me want to jump and spring.

Thea Wormald (8)

MY FAVOURITE THINGS - Simply The Best

My Favourite Things

My favourite things are all to do with Christmas.
I wake up in the morning to open my presents with my family,
As I eat my Christmas pudding.

I love the Christmas tree, as it lights up.
I love the dogs that bark outside
And the next day, when I go on holiday.
I like the snow that falls on the ground,
These are a few of my favourite things.

Dancing, singing, swimming and exploring,
Eating chocolate till I explode.
Going on Bebo and MSN,
Playing on my XBox 360 and my Nintendo DS,
Watching EastEnders and Coronation Street,
Going out with family for a lovely treat
And the way the sun is a golden coin.
These are a few of my favourite things.

Sarah Freitas (12)

Christmas Time

I can see children
Opening their Christmas presents.

I can see children
Making snowmen.

I can see children
Throwing snowballs at each other.

I love Christmas
And the snow altogether.

Joel Hall (10)

My Favourite Things

My favourite things are . . .
Playing games and beating my dad,
Being cheeky and being bad,
Christmas and Hallowe'en, they're so fun
And also playing in the sun.
These are a few of my favourite things.

Playing games with my pet,
Scoring goals in the net,
Having parties too,
Making things with paper and glue.
These are a few of my favourite things.

Eating ice cream
And sweets and treats,
Watching my favourite band sing
And having loads of songs to sing.
These are a few of my favourite things.

Samantha Foxon (11)

My Little Sister

My little sister, sweet as pie,
When it's Christmas her eyes glow like the sky.
She twinkles as the sun flames up in the sky,
I can remember when we went to Australia to see the kangaroo
And when we went to Disneyland to see Mickey Mouse's crew.
Her favourite colours are pink and red,
But mine isn't the same, they're red, pink and blue.
My little sister, sweet as pie,
When it's Christmas her eyes glow like the sky.

Kara Allen (9)

MY FAVOURITE THINGS - Simply The Best

Pets Are The Best

I like pets, they are fluffy
They wriggle and they tickle
When they sit on my tummy.

My favourite pet is a big, golden dog,
When he goes out in the fog
He plays with frogs.

He splashes in the pond
And jumps up and down
He makes a big, barking sound.

Dogs are fun
Dogs are the best
I love it when they make a mess.

My favourite thing about my golden dog
Is his big, bright eyes and warm coat
He is cosy and he is my best friend.

Olivia Rose Wanless (8)

Giraffes Are My Favourite Things

Soft coat, glinting in the sun,
While the big giraffe shatters a lion with its hooves.
But the gentle eyes shining in the blazing hot sun calm it.

Long eyelashes fluttering in the breeze,
Eyelashes like girls ponytails, swishing.

Legs like Mount Everest,
Like stilts, standing tall,
Feet as tough as tortoise shells.

Gliding through the grass,
Every so often stopping to eat, tree muncher.
Look how tall she is.
She is a skyscraper.
Amazing!

And that's why giraffes are my favourite thing.

Joya Sastry (12)

My Favourite Things

My favourite things are pink,
Pink lamp, pink jewellery, pink dress and pink pen.
All day long I think,
What else can I buy that is pink?

My favourite things are pencils and pens,
Pencils in my drawers, pens in my pencil case.
I can see them everywhere I face.

My favourite things are my books,
Poem books, story books, fiction and non-fiction books.
My gold fish can see books everywhere it looks.

My favourite things are my pictures,
Pictures that are new, pictures that are old.
Pictures have your memories is what I've been told.

My favourite things are my favourite things,
Nail polish and hairbrushes or even golden rings.

Tasnima Khan (14)

My Favourite Things

My favourite things are
Xbox games and playing in the sun .
Sleeping over at my friends is lots of fun.

My favourite things are riding my bike down to the shop,
Coming back with an icicle pop.

My favourite things are
Driving my remote control car,
I zoom round the corner,
I go fast and far.

My favourite things are
Playing golf with my dad,
I tap the ball in, hitting the flag.

These are my favourite things
And I'm glad.

Shaun Whelan (11)

MY FAVOURITE THINGS - Simply The Best

My Favourite Things

I like hugs from my dad and my mummy
Plus tasty pizza to fill my tummy.
Football is what I like the best
Even watching Johnny Test.
Playing on my scooter is what I like
And playing on my big, black bike.
Getting large presents and treats
Plus eating chocolates and sweets.
X Factor I like, that's a lot, phew!
And I like playing on my PS2.
Watching television
That definitely fills my vision.
I love playing in my garden, it's really fun
But only if I can see the yellow sun.

Thank you for reading the poem I wrote
And this is the end of my note.

Zaki Thomas (9)

A Few Of My Favourite Things

These are a few of my favourite things.
Those annoying songs that make everyone sing.
Inky black nights, all studded with stars,
Colourful sweets all wrapped up, in jars.
At school, in the playground, chatting with friends,
And never-ending games of pretend.
Being tucked up in bed, all cosy and warm,
Watching the lightning during a storm.
My mother's calm voice when I awake with a fright.
Her arms that hold me, safe and tight.
My brother's smile as he jumps on my bed,
Bedtime stories my dad has already read.
Football in the park, on a wet, muddy day,
Going outside with my sisters to play.
But my most favourite thing?
Being part of a family, bound with love, like a string.

Albert Perris (10)

My Favourite Things

Having fun and chilling out,
Going to parties in the night,
Watching TV,
Listening to CDs,
At 6pm having my tea.

Catching up with gossip, with all my mates,
Visiting the Christmas fete.
Celebrating Eid and getting money,
Going to theme parks if it's sunny.

Hanging out with all my mates at the mall,
Playing with Bratz, Barbie and Polly dolls,
Being active and reading books
And concentrating on my looks.

These are some of my favourite things,
But what I like to do most is to sing!

Ruqia Jaan (10)

The Things I Like

I like computer games and TV,
I like playing on my Nintendo Wii,
I like animals, I've got lots of pets,
Going for a check up, they don't like the vets.
I've got dogs, guinea pigs and chickens too,
Let's go on an egg hunt, that's fun for me and you.
I do lots of gymnastics, nine hours a week,
I like playing with my friends, especially hide-and-seek.
I like making necklaces and bracelets too,
Beads, string and a sewing machine, that's a fun thing to do.
Going on the computer on my MSN,
Make a mess in the bedroom building teddies their own little den.
I like getting presents and lots of little gifts,
Playing with my hair making Elvis Presley quaffs.
I like doing baking and singing to my favourite song,
I like going clothes shopping, where you can come along!

Emily Darling (11)

My Favourite Things

My favourite colour is purple
My mum's favourite is cream
My dad's favourite is blue
And my sister's favourite is green.

My favourite animal is a dolphin
My friend is a dog
My uncle's favourite is a hamster
And my grandfather's is a frog.

My favourite sport is netball
My cousin's favourite is cricket
My auntie's favourite is football
And my grandmother's is knitting.

But the one thing I like best is just to be myself.
Having my own looks, feelings, personality,
Having favourite things that are different from everyone else.

Paige Blake (13)

My Huggable Dad

When my dad gives me a hug,
I feel warm and safe.
When I am sad,
My huggable dad cheers me up.
I can give my dad a hug anytime.
I love giving my dad a hug.
I will never forget
My huggable dad's hug.
My huggable dad's hug
Is like hugging a teddy bear.
I love getting hugs
From my huggable dad.
This is my poem
About my huggable dad,
I will never forget
My huggable dad.

Shannon Gair (12)

My Favourite Things

I'm sat in my home, writing my poem,
I love to play out with my friends
And write with pens.

We play on our bikes,
'Cause it's what we like,
I like to play on my roller skates
And hula hoop and scooter too.
Hide and seek, 'cause you get those who cheat
And all they do is peek.
When it starts getting cold, me and my friend go in my bedroom
For an hour and then it's time to go.

I play with my brother before he goes to bed,
Then he goes to sleep with his favourite ted.
I then give him a goodnight kiss on his cute head.

These are my favourite things.

Georgia Rochester (9)

Happiness

Happiness is playing with my friends and family
Happiness is going to my caravan
Happiness is going on holiday
Happiness is watching TV
Happiness is going on the computer
Happiness is writing poems
Happiness is doing art and DT at school
Happiness is messing around at home
Happiness is annoying my brother
Happiness is hugging my mum and dad
Happiness is going to parties
Happiness is going on walks
Happiness is riding my bike
Happiness is getting up at the weekend
Happiness is getting some peace and quiet -
My dad says.

Samantha Lee (9)

MY FAVOURITE THINGS - Simply The Best

Reading Books

Reading is fun,
Reading is cool,
Reading books are educational,
They teach you new things, new words,
And how to be better at reading.

Reading is brilliant,
Reading is swell,
Reading can be about
Knowing the moral of the story
And how to understand it.

Reading is hip,
Reading is delightful,
When you read, you enjoy it.
I love reading,
I hope you do too!

Simone Thomas (11)

My Favourite Things

I love sleepovers,
They're really cool.
Games and scary prank makeovers too!
Midnight feasts,
Chocolates and sweets,
Spin the bottle to see whom you like least.

Making up stories
Is what I like to do,
Honest, honest, what I tell you is true!
I use princesses, kidnappers, villains and heroes,
All favourites, none voted zero.
I like to put a twist in my tale,
For my princesses - no wedding veil.

These are all of my favourite things.
These are the things that make me *ring!*

Georgina Morris (11)

Favourite Things

Friendship, family, it's all nice,
Pizza and cake - give me a slice.
Ice cream is nice, it's really cold,
I love my grandpa and he's so bold.
These are some of my favourite things.

My birthday and Hallowe'en, it's so cool,
Wow! For Christmas I got a swimming pool!
Chocolates, sweets and treats, it's all good,
For my tea a few potato spuds.
These are some of my favourite things.

Toys and games, they're so fun,
Especially when we're playing out in the sun.
Alesha Dixon, Leona too,
My brother loves them and he's only two!
These are some of my favourite things.

Nicole Olivia Dallison (9)

My Favourite Things

Listening to music and singing along,
Remembering the time I didn't know the song.
Playing my bass guitar with four strings,
Are these a few of your favourite things?

Being with friends, getting hyper playing along,
Writing poems, stories and music and songs,
Reading my favourite books by Stephanie Meyer
Spending time in the morning doing my make-up and hair
Are these a few of your favourite things?

Daydreaming about the actor, Johnny Depp,
Watching my favourite music video trying to learn the dance steps.
Watching Dunfermline Athletic play football,
They are my favourite football team,
Thinking about the man of my dreams.
Now these are a few of my favourite things.

Sarah Venters (13)

MY FAVOURITE THINGS - Simply The Best

My Favourite Things!

I like visiting my friends, it's my only dream,
While I'm there I like to eat ice cream.
I like playing in the sun,
It's so much fun.
I like, I like, I like.

I like playing with cool gadgets,
Instead of looking at horrible maggots.
I like going on holiday to see amazing places
And looking at beautiful faces.
I like, I like, I like.

I like going to fun parties
And eating chocolate Smarties.
I like playing with cats
Instead of piling mats.
These are a few of my favourite things.

Khowla Shahid (11)

Christmas

C hristmas is a time of love
H iding presents under the tree, Santa
R iding his reindeer
I cicles hanging off the roof
S anta drinking milk and eating biscuits, the
T ree with baubles on the branches
M istletoe and holly on the roof
A t Christmas Day
S itting by the fire.

Hadley Whiting (10)

My Favourite Things

These are a few of my favourite things
Like
Fruit!
I like fruit because it's fresh,
Sweet, crunchy and scrummy in my tummy.

These are a few of my favourite things
Sun!
I like sun because
On a cold day it will grow
Like a sunflower.

These are a few of my favourite things
Trampolining!
I like trampolining, because when I feel blue
I can jump to the sky and then float down.

These are a few of my favourite things
Acting!
I like acting because I can do or be
Anything I want to be.

These are a few of my favourite things.

Athen Brady
City of London School for Girls

MY FAVOURITE THINGS - Simply The Best

I Like . . .

I like reading and creative writing,
So long as it's not about fighting.
Books are fun
To read in the sun.

I like to lie on the beach,
Ice cream all round, one each.
One for Jack and one for Rose,
Now mine is on my nose.

I like my snake
But we don't feed it cake.
We feed it mice
The colour of ice.
These are a few of my favourite things,
But who knows what the future brings?

Rose Pitman-Wallace (8)
City of London School for Girls

what are your favourite things?

Write about your favourite things for our new poetry competition. Send us your poem for the chance to be published and even win your very own laptop!

PlayStation games and **playing in the sun**
Visiting friends, **parties**, **holidays** and **fun**
Camping in the garden, **catching things with wings**
Are these a few of your favourite things?

Halloween and **Christmas – presents** and **treats**
Watching TV, **eating ice cream** and **sweets**
Going to school, learning about **queens** and **kings**
Are these a few of your favourite things?

A **hug from your mum**, a **kiss from your dad too**
Making stuff out of **coloured paper** and **glue**
Dressing up as a pirate or a **princess with rings**
Are these a few of your favourite things?

Laptops and **gadgets** and **playing with your pet**
Scoring a goal in the back of the net
Babies and **robots** and **puppets with strings**
Are these a few of your favourite things?

X Factor and **reading a good book**
Doing something cheeky then let off the hook
Smiling when **Girls Aloud** or **McFly** sings
Are these a few of your favourite things?

Write your poem, then fill in your name, address and age underneath your poem, place in an envelope and send to us at: My Favourite Things, Young Writers, Remus House, Coltsfoot Drive, Woodston, Peterborough, PE2 9JX. You can email your poem instead to youngwriters@forwardpress.co.uk - don't forget to include your name, age and postal address with My Favourite Things in the subject line.